# OSSIE

## my life in football

## OSVALDO ARDILES

### with Mike Langley

SIDGWICK & JACKSON

LONDON

*First published in 1983 in Great Britain
by Sidgwick and Jackson Limited.*

*Copyright © 1983 by Osvaldo Ardiles and Mike Langley.*

*Picture research by Anne Horton.*

*ISBN 0-283-98872-X
Filmset by Green Gate Studios,
Hull, England.
Printed in Great Britain
by Biddles Ltd., Guildford, Surrey
for Sidgwick and Jackson Limited
1 Tavistock Chambers, Bloomsbury Way
London WC1A 2SG*

# CONTENTS

# LIST OF ILLUSTRATIONS

8

# 1 THE ROAD TO ENGLAND

Sixteen lanes of traffic battle night and day along Ninth of July Avenue in Buenos Aires, separated by the gardens of a small square and overlooked by an obelisk like a modern Cleopatra's Needle.

Fellow golfers will understand when I say a five-iron might be required to clear the mighty avenue from pavement to pavement because the Ninth is one of the widest roads in the world, and one of the busiest. However, on Sunday, 25 June 1978, pedestrians choked it to a standstill.

Argentina had just won the World Cup and its people took joyously to the streets, not just the millions from the capital but also visitors from the provinces who had been streaming into Buenos Aires for days, some of them clinging to the sides of overcrowded trains and others crammed into sagging, battered cars. They overflowed from the great boulevard and into the shopping precinct, but the swirling crowd was at its thickest and noisiest outside the Plaza Hotel which was the venue for the team's victory banquet.

I was in the midst of the crowd but trying to be invisible; wearing dark glasses, I crouched in the back of a police car and, for extra protection, I covered my face with my hands. The fans meant me no harm, of course, but their excitement and the sheer number of them made them an unpredictable force even though they seemed content just dancing and singing. They never tired of waving the national flag with its bands of pale blue (for our vast sky) and silver (for the precious metal that gave Argentina its name), but their real desire was to see and touch the footballers who had conquered the

9

world. I was one of those, although the realization hadn't fully sunk in.

We had beaten Holland 3–1 after extra time at River Plate stadium but the events immediately afterwards are blurred in my memory. We all seemed in a rush – showering, changing, packing, and pausing only briefly to pay attention when General Jorge Rafael Videla, the President of Argentina, came in with several of his ministers to congratulate us. There were bottles of champagne but we didn't open them. We weren't in a party mood but preoccupied and solemn, even a little stunned in that first hour after the final. It was much later that I began to savour our achievement, and I think the others were the same.

I was more concerned at the time about my wife, Sylvia, who was six months pregnant with my second son Federico and had stayed at home to avoid the crowds. I had to hurry home to escort her to the banquet. Three of us (myself, Ricky Villa and Norberto Alonso) lived on the same side of Buenos Aires and we shared a police car from the ground, but even with the assistance of a second police car, its siren blaring, the two-mile journey home was slow through the throng.

It was obvious that the city centre would be jammed solid so I asked the neighbourhood police for transport to the banquet instead of attempting to drive myself. Argentinian police are normally second to none at clearing a path through crowds. They seal off streets, turn all the lights to green and send motorcycle outriders ahead to sweep aside motorists in their way – but that wild Sunday evening defeated even the police and our last 600 yards to the Plaza were no faster than a funeral march.

We might never have reached the hotel but for spotting an ambulance, the only vehicle to which the crowds gave way. Our driver tucked in behind the ambulance and stuck to its rear bumper as it advanced like a snowplough. I lowered myself below the car windows until I was almost sitting on the floor. In that way, we arrived at the banquet. The five-mile journey had taken two hours.

Just as the final itself is a blur in my memory, I have only the most general impression of the dinner that followed. There were speeches by President Videla and João Havelange, the F.I.F.A. president. I remember going to the top table for my winner's medal and applauding two extra presentations to Mario Kempes who had been a boy star with me in Córdoba. Kempes was awarded a golden boot as the

World Cup's highest scorer with six goals and another trophy for being voted 'Man of the Tournament'.

The function ended at about one in the morning and by British standards would be classed, I suppose, as a remarkably sober affair. Latins – perhaps particularly Argentinians – are moderate drinkers. Our pleasure derives from company and conversation and, although we stayed around the hotel chatting until nearly dawn, none of the players drank more than a few glasses of wine in all that time. I slipped away to a telephone in the small hours and called my parents and brothers in Córdoba, saying: 'I'll be home with you today, just as soon as I can get a plane.'

Córdoba is Argentina's second largest city; a million people live there but news flashes through the streets as quickly as in a village and so I landed to a hero's welcome. It seemed as if the entire population had turned out and my father's house was under siege.

The fans wanted a handshake or an autograph, or both. Many of them were happy just to be near me – to see me, to touch my jacket and pat me on the back. I enjoyed all the attention I was getting but at the same time it was tiring and I said to my father: 'Any celebrations are best held here at home. It's going to be impossible to take me into a restaurant. We'd be mobbed.'

When the initial fuss died down and it was possible to eat out again, the restaurants refused to let me pay. The same thing happened in shops; as one of the heroes of Argentina, I could have had all I wanted free. Fiat gave me a car, as they did to the rest of the team, and small gifts from well-wishers arrived by the score, along with thousands of cards and letters. Yet even while basking in the warmth of Córdoba's welcome, I knew that my footballing days in Argentina were numbered.

I played for the Huracán club in Buenos Aires and they were nearly broke; only the sale of a World Cup player could save them and that narrowed the field to three names. There was the brilliant winger, Rene Houseman, one of the best footballers I've ever seen, although he hadn't been quite at his peak in the World Cup, then there was Hector Baley, Argentina's No. 2 goalkeeper, but he had made no appearances in the tournament and it was doubtful whether a 'keeper could command a big enough fee. So that left me; I had missed only one match in the World Cup – and that through injury – and I was eager to try my luck in Europe, especially after touring there with Argentina in 1976.

*World Cup winners! Skipper Daniel Passarella holds the golden trophy high after Argentina's 3–1 victory against Holland in the 1978 final at River Plate stadium in Buenos Aires. I am next to Passarella on the right, numbered 2 on my shorts and with my face half-hidden by the arms of substitute Omar Larrosa*

Huracán played in Patricios Park, which is about as close to the city centre as, say, Chelsea's ground is to the West End. And, like Chelsea in the last few years, Huracán had been known mainly for their struggles.

Then in 1971 César Luis Menotti became manager and revolutionized their playing style. He preached skill instead of the physical, often violent, football that was becoming the trademark of successful South American teams – the 'Libertadores Cup', South America's equivalent to the European Cup, for example, produced a series of battles. And when the eventual winners met the European champions in the world club championship final, the result was usually a head-on collision. For instance, six players were sent off in a decider between Racing of Argentina and Glasgow Celtic in 1967, and the following year was notorious for two brawls between Manchester United and Estudiantes de la Plata, another Argentinian club.

Estudiantes stretched footballing laws to the limit, and in doing so had been very successful. They reached three successive world club finals. Teams began to copy them. Menotti was derided as a romantic dreamer but soon proved the contrary by guiding Huracán to the Argentina championship. He resigned in December 1974 to become the national manager but left behind a team that was playing the most entertaining football to be seen in Buenos Aires when I joined them in 1975. We were runners-up, but moral champions, the following year; that's not only my opinion, it was the opinion of virtually everyone – an unlucky 1–0 defeat by Boca Juniors on a wet pitch cost us the title and gave Boca the championship.

Menotti, the man who made Huracán, was also their downfall. He used his power to conscript star players for his national squad, taking them away for months if he wished, while the clubs were left to fend for themselves as best they could. In Huracán's case, that meant sinking into the middle of the table without Houseman, Baley and me to help them in the World Cup year of 1978.

Argentina is second only to Brazil in its passion for football. Brazil comes first because suicide is a frequent Brazilian response to defeat. Although Argentinians live for the game, they are rarely mad enough to die for it.

The other side of Argentinian fervour is impatience. Our teams cannot count on those solid bodies of loyal supporters who stick by English clubs through the bad times. For instance, Huracán, when challenging for the title, drew crowds of 30,000; out of the running the club averaged only 10,000 and that's why they were short of money.

They phoned me in Córdoba a few days after the final.

'You're going to Spain,' they said. A few clubs were mentioned, none definitely.

I said: 'Spain, France or Italy are all the same to me because I've played in Europe with the national side. I'll like it wherever I go.'

England wasn't mentioned. No Argentinian had played in Britain to the best of my knowledge and so the idea of joining an English club hadn't occurred to me. To my great surprise, Huracán phoned a week later with the news: 'It's all arranged. You're going to Manchester City and Ricky Villa is going with you.' Then came the financial details.

'O.K.,' I said. 'No problem. I'll catch the first plane to Buenos Aires.' We arranged to meet in the Libertador Hotel.

I bought a map of England on the way to the airport and measured the distance between Manchester and London. I had heard of Manchester United but not of City. United, Arsenal and Liverpool were the only English clubs that I could name in those days. I had never heard of Tottenham Hotspur, so there was a surprise waiting for me when I reached the Libertador Hotel.

'Osvaldo,' they said, drawing me aside, 'it's not Manchester now, it's Tottenham,' adding, when they saw my blank look, 'It's O.K., it's in London.'

The Libertador had become the temporary headquarters of Harry Haslam – Happy Harry – then the manager of Sheffield United and the first Briton to realize the potential of a transfer trade with the hard-up Argentinian clubs. He was a bluff, jovial figure and, I discovered later, a popular speaker at men-only football dinners in England. In his home country he was also known as a shrewd operator in the transfer market. His club was in the Second Division playing to average crowds of about 15,000 – and yet here he was on the other side of the world stealing a march on all his richer and bigger rivals by trying to sign Diego Maradona, only seventeen then, for £400,000. The negotiations came to nothing in the end because Harry's directors felt unable to raise the cash for what would have been a record fee for them. Even if they had decided to go ahead, Sheffield United would certainly have been outbid eventually or would have found that the export of Maradona was prohibited by the Argentinian F.A. So instead Harry concentrated on alerting other English clubs to the availability of myself and Ricky Villa.

Harry was well informed about Argentinian football because Sheffield United had South American connections. The assistant manager, Danny Bergara, was from Uruguay and one of the coaches was Oscar Arce, an Argentinian who had played some games for Aston Villa and worked with the youth team at Millwall. Oscar was a close friend of Tony Rattin, Argentina's World Cup captain in 1966. Rattin is enshrined in the record books as the first footballer to be sent off at Wembley for persistent arguing and dissent in the quarter-final against England.

Arce, I suppose, was the key to the affair in that he helped to pick out transfer targets and acted as interpreter. He was in the room with Harry Haslam when I arrived. The two of them then ushered in a tall, quiet man who looked down at me and said reassuringly 'Everything is going to be all right. We'll take care of you and Ricky, and of your wives'.

Harry had introduced him as Keith Burkinshaw, the manager of Tottenham Hotspur, and I sensed as he talked that he was trying to gauge my personality. Football wasn't mentioned. It wasn't necessary because he was familiar with my play, but he knew nothing about my character. He asked questions about my family and background to give him an idea of my outlook and attitude. He was trying to study me, and I was doing the same with him. He struck me as an honest man and so I signed – for a club I had never heard of in a country I hadn't thought about, and only a fortnight after being acclaimed a hero of Argentina.

It was a gamble for me and a bigger gamble for Keith, whose team was newly promoted to the First Division and in need of a daring signing to convince its supporters that the club was determined to stay there. Neither of us guessed how splendidly this mutual gamble would repay our highest hopes.

*Keith Burkinshaw struck me as an honest man and so I signed for Tottenham Hotspur, a club I had never heard of in a country I hadn't thought about. It was a gamble for me and an even bigger gamble for Keith*

# 2 STREET FOOTBALL TO NATIONAL SIDE

I was a street footballer in Córdoba from the age of five, kicking a ball around with the bigger boys while the girls kept watch for cars. I played with bigger boys because there were never any smaller ones. Every boy in the neighbourhood towered over me and I often needed the support of my elder brothers to overcome the objection: 'Osvaldo can't play. He's too little.' My boyhood and early teens were a long fight against such snap judgments: 'Too frail, too tiny, too easy to kick off the ball. Can't play!'

At home I faced a different type of discouragement from my parents. My father and mother didn't say that I couldn't play but that I shouldn't play – at least, not so much. My father is highly intelligent and I'm very close to him, never letting a week slip by without phoning home. In my heart I knew he was right to regard football as a risky and unreliable occupation. He longed for me to follow him into law instead of being a madcap who played football all day and then in the evenings under a street lamp kicked a tennis ball against the wall.

Football, football, football! Nothing else was in my head and my father's fears for me were quietened only by a steady stream of excellent school reports and examination marks; this wasn't due to any excessive zeal on my part, but simply the result of a natural aptitude for studying.

So my father let me pursue the sporting life, which was easy enough as we lived close to a sports complex where I swam, played tennis, and even basketball, and won the Córdoba under-eighteen table-tennis championship. But there was no contest when it came to choosing between these other activities and football. I'd had a dream since the day I had first kicked a ball: to play for Argentina. I never forgot that dream.

Argentina has no equivalent to the English Schools Football Association; in fact, the game is not played in schools because the educationists know that football's immense popularity guarantees ample opportunity for it outside, and so they encourage the children to play other games – tennis and handball, for instance. This means that every Argentinian footballer starts playing in the streets – and why not? After all, that was the birthplace of the game with entire English villages turning out to kick the ball (and often each other) down the rutted market streets and muddy lanes.

My brothers, Arturo and Guillermo encouraged me. Arturo (named after my father and, like him, a lawyer) was a fine player himself, reaching the fringes of First Division football before a knee injury ended his career.

Guillermo, who is in business now, was my closest brother although we are as different as chalk and cheese in many ways. It was because of affection for Guillermo that I signed for Instituto Córdoba as an amateur. I turned a deaf ear to accusations of 'little traitor' from Córdoba Juniors, another First Division club, who had expected me to register with them. Córdoba Juniors, regarded me as their property because I lived in their part of the city and used their swimming pool and tennis courts. However, Guillermo was an Instituto fan and kept reminding me: 'Juniors is more of a social club than a football club. Instituto have the best football set-up and you've got to go for the best.' At seventeen I was in their first team and once in, never out. At first I played just for appearance money and bonuses but, at nineteen, I signed a full professional contract with Instituto.

The foundation of my success with them had been laid while playing for an amazingly successful boy's side called Red Star – so called as a tribute to the famous Yugoslavian club after their impressive playing visit to Córdoba. Between the ages of seven and sixteen, I played for various Red Star teams, winning 150 medals in the process. I played for them in five-a-side, six-a-side, seven-a-side and eight-a-side matches. I didn't become eligible for a full eleven-a-side team until I was fifteen because height was a determining factor in selection for what Argentinians term 'baby football'. They said I was too small and, being only four feet six inches tall at the age of thirteen I couldn't argue.

Youth football, the next step up from baby football, is thoroughly organized in Argentina, and Instituto were champions of all the six youth divisions in my time. I could play every Sunday morning for an Instituto team and every evening for Red Star, being still below the baby football height limit of one-and-a-half metres (about five feet).

It was in one of these evening games that I first ran across Mario Kempes who was playing for Bell Ville, a small town some 100 miles from Córdoba. We beat them 6–0 and I didn't even notice Kempes. However, he remembered me and reminded me of the result at our next meeting some years later when he signed for Instituto. He was then almost eighteen and I was an established first-teamer aged twenty.

Although my football career was progressing rapidly, I still heeded my father's advice: 'Educate yourself. You could be so much more than just a good footballer.' He knew that the odds were stacked against success in professional sport. I could see that for myself. Many boys as talented as I had started off with me in baby football only to fall by the wayside.

Steve Coppell took his degree at Liverpool University while continuing to play throughout Manchester United's run to the 1976 F.A. Cup final, so he would understand how I was able to combine football with law studies. There was never a spare minute but it was fun nevertheless. I reported to Córdoba University at half-past seven most mornings, then drove to train with Instituto at ten-thirty, returning to college for evening studies.

Everything seemed to happen fast on that breakneck timetable: I learned to play chess; I worked on improving the touch-typing that I first took up during my early teens with the intention of giving my father more secretarial help; I learned to drive; I bought a house while still a student and only twenty years old. Also, I married Sylvia. We first met when I was eighteen, being introduced by a friend. All I said then was 'Encantada' – literally, 'Enchanted' – which might sweep the girls off their feet in English but is no more than 'Hello' to a lady in Spanish. We met again at university where she was also studying law and our relationship became more serious.

Somehow in this blur of activity I even fitted in my year of compulsory military service and became Soldier Osvaldo César Ardiles of the Argentinian Air Force. I had dreaded conscription

*Me at the age of eleven when playing for Red Star (Córdoba). I won 150 medals while playing for the various Red Star teams between the ages of seven and sixteen*

but found myself enjoying it; nothing unpleasant happened to me apart from the camp barber shaving my head to the bone on the first day. I enlisted at New Year 1973, which meant that my basic training was completed in football's close season. I had two months of drill, patrols, assault courses, war exercises and a couple of guard duties before being sent to the non-commissioned officers school with my little forage cap at the approved angle.

I was found a job as an office messenger and given ample time to play football and keep in training. A conscript's pay is nominal, just enough to cover coffee and biscuits in the canteen and meet the small charges for the endless games of pool and table tennis, but as a footballer I earned more than many of the regular officers. Conveniently, too, I was never posted outside Córdoba or required to sleep in the camp after the completion of basic training; I could live like a lord at home. The football honours began arriving after my demob. First, I was selected to play for a team representing the province of Córdoba and for a national tournament in Buenos Aires where I was voted 'Best Player from the Interior of Argentina'. The award launched me into the big-time by bringing my name to the notice of the metropolitan clubs. Sure enough, a buyer from Buenos Aires soon appeared.

I had enjoyed the lyrical football that Kempes and I had been able to play together at Córdoba in an all-international attack, but a place with Huracán, recent champions and still strong contenders, was an opportunity not to be missed. When they offered what was then a record fee, neither Instituto nor I hesitated about accepting.

Huracán's ground was one of the best in Buenos Aires, ranking only slightly behind River Plate and Vélez Sarsfield, the capital's two World Cup venues in 1978. I knew that joining Huracán would interfere with my studies because they sometimes trained twice a day and always spent at least one night in what Latin footballers call 'concentration'. This is really a fancy name for booking the whole team into a hotel and stopping the dressing-room Romeos from slipping off with girls!

Even if I had been able to fit a degree course round the club's schedule, law and football would have proved an impossible combination once I was chosen for the national team; that realization was not long in coming and even though it meant postponing my studies for a few years, I was nevertheless thrilled at the prospect.

My first task at Huracán was to establish my right to a place in the side, as there was no immediate opening for me. I'm a right-sided player whose best position in on the right of midfield, but those places were already filled by two stars from the 1974 World Cup in West Germany. They were Carlos Alberto Babington and Miguel Angel Brindisi. The No. 8 and No. 10 shirts (as Argentinians number the right of midfield) were their property so I made my début wearing No. 9, much to the mystification of the spectators. Fannessi, one of the club's most experienced players, asked me afterwards: 'Do you know what should be on your back?'

'An eight or a ten. Maybe an eleven,' I said.

Fannessi pounced: 'Wrong! You ought to wear a question mark because no one knows where you're supposed to be.'

I wasn't upset. There was a lot of sense in what he said as I was aware of being a paradox as a right-sided player who feels more comfortable on the left and most of all likes to roam the pitch.

When my pay cheque arrived a month late, I knew Huracán were typical of the Argentinian clubs that live beyond their means. In my experience, this is nearly all of them apart from River Plate, Ferro, Independiente and Vélez Sarsfield. They get into a financial muddle by agreeing to pay out more in wages than they take in gate receipts. At the same time they run up enormous expenses for 'concentration'; indeed, some managers, not satisfied with locking up their team for almost a week before a match, keep their players in the hotel even after the match is over. Much of the expenditure is unnecessary, especially before home games. I'm sure the English way is far better; when a player is able to spend the eve of a game with his family he feels more natural and relaxed.

Anyway, the result of the clubs' over-spending is a constant stream of bouncing cheques and broken promises. My salary has often been two months late. After complaining, I've been given cheques that the bank refused to honour. Further protests are futile because they'll only be met by some official shrugging disarmingly while saying: 'Oh, well. Maybe tomorrow.' And I was one of the stars!

The wage range for Argentinian footballers is much broader than in England. For instance, a first team player at Rochdale is a good deal closer in salary to Kevin Keegan than a lower division Argentinian would be to Diego Maradona. Quite often, the small-time player in Argentina can think himself lucky to be paid at all.

Huracán's money troubles coincided with rampant inflation.

World Cup visitors to Buenos Aires may remember the many advertisements offering interest of ninety per cent a year on bank deposits. The rate seemed sensational to Europeans, yet even on ninety per cent – and despite the government's efforts to control inflation – the saver would lose in the long run.

There was one way for footballers to end the uncertainties surrounding their pay packets and that was to win a regular place in the national team. Top players in Argentina were always all right; no matter who else went without, the internationals would be paid.

I wasn't long in joining their élite group although the transfer to Huracán had meant several adjustments for me. For a start, my new club was far more professional than Instituto, and the Buenos Aires league was of a higher standard. It also housed many defenders raised in the old tradition of the body-check and blocking knee. They looked at me and thought what opponents have been thinking all my life: 'Too small.' In fact, I'm as tall as Kevin Keegan and my fragile appearance is very deceptive.

English players may find it hard to believe, but I must say that playing in Argentinian football is less dangerous than playing in the First Division. For instance (and I think these figures could be repeated throughout the Football League), twenty-five of the forty professionals at Tottenham have undergone at least one operation during their careers. Serious injuries are rarer in Argentina, largely because of the better playing conditions. We play in sunshine, not in the rain, partly to conserve the pitches but chiefly because, as the grounds are uncovered, the crowds wouldn't come. We don't run the risk of knee and ankle damage that afflicts English players turning on bad pitches, or the fractures that happen so often in Britain as a result of collisions on ice.

My full international call-up came as a pleasure but not a surprise because I already knew I was being considered for selection. Menotti, Argentina's manager, had picked me twice previously for representative matches with the Interior XI while I was at Instituto, so I felt confident that he would continue to discount my lack of inches and remain true to his belief that 'Ability at football is not a question of height, weight, slimness or sturdiness. Above all, it is a question of intelligence.'

Menotti wanted me for a European tour in the spring of 1976. It was to visit Russia, Poland, Hungary, West Germany and Spain. I felt at ease in Europe from the very start, even in Kiev with the snow, the first sizeable fall I had seen, piled shoulder-high along the touchlines. Europe is the goal of every educated Argentinian. It was dear to me also as the continent of my ancestors – Spanish on my father's side, Italian on my mother's.

We won in Russia and in Poland, lost in West Berlin and drew in Seville. We lost 2–0 in Budapest where home defeats are a rarity; for example, England's 3–1 victory at the Nep stadium in June 1981 was their first in Hungary since 1909. So the scoreline against us was not too bad and it concealed an impressive performance by Argentina, particularly by Kempes, but we just could not get the ball in the net, and also let in their second goal in the closing minutes. Menotti was pleased with us and the significance of our performance was not lost on the referee who said afterwards: 'I've just seen the next world champions. Not Hungary, but Argentina.'

# 3 MENOTTI

César Luis Menotti, like so many managers, wanted a team that would be almost exactly the opposite of himself as a player. He was the dressing-room rebel who insisted on total obedience, the languid artist who demanded ever-increasing effort, the noted gambler who prohibited even penny stakes in our card schools.

I met him for the first time in February 1975 when he had been Argentina's national manager for just a month and when, with only lukewarm public support in a notoriously insecure post, he was not expected to keep his job until the end of the year.

'Express yourself, enjoy yourself. I just want to see you play,' he said before my debut with his Interior XI, adding what had always been considered heresy: 'Don't worry about the result.'

He was only thirty-five, unusually young to run a major World Cup side, but widely experienced for his age: he had twenty-five international caps as a midfield creator and one league championship as a club manager. He also knew foreign football, having played in the São Paulo league in Brazil and spent two years with New York Generals under Freddie Goodwin, a former manager of Brighton and of Birmingham City. Menotti showed North America that he was rightly renowned as one of the hardest shots in Argentina because Goodwin remembers: 'We called him "Cannonball". Once, quite incredibly, he scored from five yards inside our half!'

For a man of six feet two inches, Menotti was exceptionally skilful. Perhaps he was sometimes too skilful for his team's good because he had a reputation for deriving more pleasure from performing some audacious trick like nutmegging an opponent – that is, flicking the ball between his legs – than he would from scoring.

Menotti and I hit it off from the start. I'm his player. He made me, shaping a World Cup winner from someone who might easily have remained a big name only in Córdoba. When I had possession at Instituto, I tended to position myself in the middle of the pitch; when the opposition had the ball, I waited for someone to retrieve it for me. That wasn't good enough for Menotti. He began developing my team sense and improving my positional play.

'Sacrifice a little individuality,' he urged. 'Make yourself the fulcrum of the team. You can play on either side so I shan't restrict you in that respect, but whatever side you're on, you must balance the others. Make yourself the fifth forward when we attack, and the extra defender helping Gallego when we lose the ball.'

This extra involvement paid off immediately. I became a better player, more industrious, and more aware; as a result, early in 1978, I found myself in Argentina's World Cup training camp. Only three of us had made it all the way from that first Interior XI – myself, Daniel Valencia and Ricky Villa.

The camp was in Mar del Plata, the seaside resort of Buenos Aires although some 250 miles from the capital. It belonged to an order of Marist priests and was used as a college and, in the holidays, as a camp for schoolchildren. There were school parties staying in the camp during our training. They watched our practice matches on the camp's six pitches and attended Mass with us in the Order's small church. Our sleeping quarters, a large chalet in the grounds, were kept completely private, sealed off from supporters and fellow-campers by anti-terrorist guards.

Two months there afforded ample opportunity to study Menotti and his enormous consumption of cigarettes. We estimated his intake at eighty a day. I found him a man of strong principles and at times inflexible, but mostly he was willing to listen to criticism provided it was kept inside the camp – a rule that no one dared break. He was amusing in private and far less reserved than his public image suggested. He was full of little stories about his playing career. That listless air was another illusion; we found him full of life and nutmeg-mad in the five-a-sides. Don't ever take on Menotti in five-a-side football because he is impossible to beat. It's not only that he plays to win but that he plays until he wins, so games go on and on until his side are in front. I've known five-a-sides at the camp last until after dusk and if the leading side dared to return to the chalet for dinner, Menotti would remain on the pitch claiming: 'You've retired, so we're the winners.'

He was just the same when his first team played the reserve team, as Argentina always do for forty minutes two days before an international match. It's an oddity of football that reserve teams anywhere often win this kind of match because they want to prove something while the first-teamers may be more concerned with avoiding injury and saving themselves for the real match. Menotti, though, refuses to countenance defeat for his first team. He likes them to score a quick goal and show some class, then he will probably stop the game after only fifteen minutes, saying: 'That'll do. Everyone back for a bath.'

Woe betide the first team, though, if they do not win. He'll keep them on the pitch until they do. In Rosario during the World Cup even that failed to achieve the desired result. The reserves won 2–0, overcoming the blatant bias of an increasingly irritated referee – Menotti himself.

'Replay tomorrow,' he ordered eventually, which was unusual because the day before a match is normally one of complete relaxation for Argentinian players. I hadn't played for the defeated first team as I was injured, but Menotti told me: 'I want you there.'

'I can't turn out without an injection,' I replied.

'Have one then,' said Menotti. 'But just a little one because I'll only need you for fifteen minutes.'

I played and we reversed the result, giving a display that convinced Menotti that there was no further need to experiment with his line-up. He fielded that second day's eleven against Brazil and in the World Cup final. He didn't burden us in either match with a lot of tactical detail about the opposition because he prefers to praise players as much as possible. He'll talk differently to every player but always with the purpose of building confidence. 'You're the best,' he says continuously and convincingly, and he backs up his words by remaining loyal to players who might be suffering a long run of poor form.

His faith was infectious. We all believed that we were the best team in the world and, by implication, were playing for the world's best boss. We didn't call him 'boss'. Menotti, like Keith Burkinshaw, has no time for titles. His style is informal, with everyone on Christian name terms. I was always 'Osvaldo' to him. For his part, he would

*César Luis Menotti, World Cup-winning manager of Argentina and a chain-smoking visionary who is unbeatable at five-a-side football*

say 'Call me César' even to the rawest recruit – and there were plenty of those in the early days when he was scouring Argentina for a side.

Our country had produced some of football's greatest players – above all, Alfredo di Stefano of Real Madrid – but had never won the World Cup or progressed further than the quarter-finals since the Second World War. One problem was the constant change in direction. No manager before Menotti had been able to keep his post for the full four years between World Cups. It was the same story before the 1974 World Cup in West Germany when the manager changed only three months before the squad left for Europe. Omar Sivori, who had been a team-mate of the great Welshman John Charles at Juventus in the 1960s, quarrelled with the Argentinian F.A. and resigned. His successor, Ladislao Cap, hardly had time to assess the players before the World Cup began. Consequently the results were even worse than anyone had feared. Argentina played six matches in Germany but won only one of them – and that was against Haiti.

Fear of a similar disaster in 1978 strengthened Menotti's hand in negotiating a contract that gave him immense authority, which he was not afraid to use. He threatened to resign after only a few months to force a showdown over the availability of players for the national team. Menotti announced a four-year plan, determined to overcome the old failings of over-reliance on individual stars and insufficient preparation for the team. Argentina suffered from a slow, short-passing style and a surplus of *prima donna* footballers who were too easily thrown out of their stride by any bad bounce. Get-togethers were rare; they were also too brief and lacked continuity because the managers and training staff changed too often. Menotti saw that nothing could be achieved without stability, both in the office and in the dressing-room.

'Why is it,' he asked, 'that hardly anyone plays thirty times for Argentina when Europe is full of footballers with fifty caps or more?'

He sent his assistants to study European coaching and training methods and asked for detailed reports on England, West Germany, Italy and Spain. Scouts were sent all over Argentina – and it is a huge country stretching more than 2,000 miles from sugar plantations in the north almost to the southern ice-cap. Menotti's men looked everywhere for talented players worth a trial in his new Interior and Youth teams. A hundred names came back to him, mine among them. Gallego, Tarantini, Passarella, Valencia and

30

Kempes were also unearthed by the network.

An enormous programme of sixty-three team-building matches was arranged, forty-six of them full international fixtures – and the caps came thick and fast. In only three years I played thirty-five international matches, which is as many appearances as Angel Labruna, a famous River Plate inside-left of the fifties, achieved in sixteen seasons.

Menotti's staff in those early days was concerned with work-rate. There was a deep-seated fear of European footballers. They seemed bigger and stronger, able to run further. We were all checked for effort by a panel of match-recorders. I came top of the class in a match against West Germany with figures that astonished even me: 100 touches of the ball and five miles of running! An official announcement described this as 'higher attainment than outstanding midfield players in Europe'.

The process of sifting and checking went on for two years until Menotti decided he'd found the basis for a new Argentina. From then on, he handled all the coaching personally.

I know there are those in England who imagine that South American footballers develop naturally without coaching. That is not the case. I was coached from the age of eight; we all are.

Roberto Cemino was my first coach. He's not famous but no one, except Menotti, has had more influence on my game. Cemino was the youth coach of Red Star and of Córdoba Instituto, a man with a deep understanding of football who devoted all his time to it. I was under his guidance for nearly ten years; the greatest lesson I learned from him was how to behave. He was too wise to burden a small boy with technicalities. He could see that I had talent and didn't need to be told what to do with the ball. His advice dealt mostly with attitudes: 'Don't sulk or flounce if I leave you out. Don't be cheeky to older people. Try to be modest, and don't get big-headed. Don't lose your temper if you're fouled, and be more unselfish; remember, it's a team game.'

Saturday is the big night in Argentina for teenage parties and dances and there was no shortage of invitations for the young lions of Red Star. Cemino always urged moderation, saying: 'If you're going to be successful on the field, you'll have to sacrifice some social life. Saturday can't be a big night when you're playing for me on Sunday morning.'

The round trip from Córdoba to Buenos Aires and back is about

800 miles. From time to time Cemino, with the club paying for the petrol, would get out his car and drive a select few of us to the capital to watch the big clubs, River Plate and Boca Juniors. As football education goes, it was unbeatable.

I was lucky to be coached by Cemino and Menotti for there were two schools of coaching in Argentina and they both belonged to the one that suited a short fellow like me. One set of coaches, such as Juan Carlos Lorenzo, aped European football and put the emphasis on pace, physical output and bodily contact. I've played for coaches with such ideas; the result was that so much time was spent on becoming super-fit that there was hardly any left for ball work. We'd see the ball only once a week, apart from matches. The Menotti-Cemino school, while acknowledging the need for fitness and effort, said: 'Nothing is more important than skill with the ball.'

There's a general belief that English coaches spend all their time turning out marathon runners rather than footballers. I've not found it so. I've seen more of the ball when training under Keith Burkinshaw and his assistant, Peter Shreeves, than I have under several coaches at Instituto and Huracán. I'm pleased with English coaching and have no complaints except about practising throw-ins. In my opinion, not very much can be achieved with a throw. But Tottenham's staff leave us scope for invention during matches; we're not over-programmed.

There's another myth that English teams spend all week practising free kicks. Perhaps a few do; if so, they're not alone. Argentina spent a lot of time on set-piece rehearsals with three routines each for four dead-ball kickers – Ortis, Passarella, Kempes and Olguin. Every team in the world has set-piece drills and signals – perhaps a raised left arm for an intended cross to the far post, a right arm for the near post, and both arms raised to indicate a direct attempt. I was Argentina's toucher, standing over the ball and asking the kicker: 'What do you want? A little roll, or nothing at all?' The answer was always off the top of the head; we weren't restricted by rigid drills.

The danger of over-elaborate free kicks had been brought home to us in a match when I rolled the ball and two or three team-mates darted away on dummy runs, without anyone actually having a shot. Confusion turned into embarrassment when the opposition stole the ball and began an attack!

Perhaps the main difference between English and Argentinian coaching can be seen in the development of schoolboy players. Men like Cemino never bothered us with tactics or systems; they didn't talk about right-sided or left-sided players. They just encouraged us to master the ball. Up to the age of twelve, the only coaching I received was on ball skills; I'd spend hours, whole afternoons even, flicking a big ball, medium ball, or, best of all, a tennis ball, trying to keep it up for 200 kicks. And our games were played on good surfaces, usually on open-air basketball courts, and were kept to five-a-side. No ploughing through mud for us without space to turn and dribble.

I feel sorry for small boys in England playing on big pitches, wasting their energy trying to move the ball over distances beyond their capabilities. They don't learn ball skills, they don't learn how to use a ball. All they learn is how to kick it a long way. I'm convinced that English football would reap immense benefits if schools restricted under-fourteen teams to small pitches and matches of no more than six a side.

This basic requirement of skill with the ball, first drummed into me by Cemino, was also the essence of Menotti's message. His championship success with Huracán was like the dawn after a long, dark night for Argentinian football. Diehards scoffed at his idea of winning attractively and fairly, but he tried to ignore them whilst he got on with the job of ensuring that we saw things his way.

'Go forward, always forward,' he'd tell us. 'It's a game of space. Find that space, then attack from it.'

Sometimes he would swipe at the Europeans, saying: 'The English and the Germans run too much and think too little. With you, it's the other way round but it's going to be easier for me to make you run than for the European coaches to teach their players to think.'

He trained us twice a day and at team talks he gave us more ideas about football, saying, for example: 'Although I want you fitter, I don't want you dashing round in a whirl for ninety minutes at the expense of your artistry and special skills. If we're going to win the World Cup, it'll have to be with specialists rather than with mere athletes. You saw what happened to the Dutch in the 1974 final at Munich. They fielded their team of total footballers, men who believed they could play in any position. But a specialist finisher, Gerd Muller of Germany, beat them.'

Menotti worked us hard in camp, but we were never bored. There was always something to do and the twice-daily training that I disliked at club level was a pleasure when the facilities were on the doorstep. No one chased us out of bed in the mornings; we could lie in as long as we liked provided we were at the training pitch by ten. We would train until lunch, eat, and then have a siesta before the second session on the training ground.

Time flowed by gently and peacefully, filled with practice matches, dead-ball routines, the odd hour on the massage table, sitting around talking, reading, watching T.V., playing tennis, table-tennis, chess, billiards and cards. We used to have card tournaments, like English whist drives, but the prizes were never more valuable than records or books. This was rather ironic at a place like Mar del Plata which is the site of the world's biggest casino. It is a veritable palace of roulette tables with more than seventy in one room, I believe.

Menotti liked the tables himself but he absolutely forbade gambling in the camp, saying: 'You start playing for a few *pesos* and you think there's no problem, but before you know where you are the bets have grown bigger and the player taking the money is no longer your friend.'

Menotti did not want to risk any damage to friendships; his camp was designed to build and strengthen bonds between the players. Integration is the purpose of the prolonged training favoured by Argentina and Brazil. It works, there's no doubt of that. We were closer than brothers after two months together. We could pick up each other's trains of thought, accurately guess each other's reaction to any emergency, knew exactly how everyone in the team wanted the ball and where he might be at any moment in a match. If anything went wrong in a match we knew we wouldn't be looking blankly at each other or holding conferences; instead, we were confident we would respond instantly.

The camp was no prison. We could go out for weekends in the early stages, or invite our families in. The bar wasn't shut and we could have wine with all our meals. As I've said, Argentinian footballers are such light drinkers that the team doctor complained: 'You're not drinking enough wine. Get it down you; it'll do you more good than coke and those other gassy drinks you like.'

A compromise was reached when the squad told the doctor: 'We're not keen on wine and you disapprove of coke, so we'll have orange juice instead.'

There were twenty-five players in camp but the World Cup rules allowed each country only twenty-two. The reduction had to be

34

made ten days before the opening match. It would be hard to find a plainer example of how cruel the game can be. Three players who had lived, trained and prepared with us for months would have their hopes dashed at the last minute. One such player is now the world's No. 1 footballer, Diego Maradona.

I suppose it was the first setback of a career than had been laid with a red carpet all the way – First Division star at fifteen, a full international only a year later, and in the World Cup reckoning at seventeen. Then Menotti discarded him. 'Too young,' he said.

A year later in Switzerland I played with Maradona against Holland in a repeat of the World Cup final to mark F.I.F.A.'s anniversary. In that year Maradona had grown into greatness. He outshone us all.

Luckily, I was not worried about selection because Menotti had long ago promised about a dozen of us (goalkeeper, Fillol, skipper, Passarella, Kempes and myself among them) that we would be in the World Cup. Menotti was a man of his word and would never go back on that undertaking, so we were free from the worries that kept the six or seven fringe players, Maradona among them, scrapping for the few spare places.

We won the World Cup without him and so I wouldn't like to start arguing that Menotti was wrong to leave him out; on the contrary, he was probably right to decide he was too young, but it must have been a most difficult choice knowing that Maradona was improving daily and playing marvellously in training.

Maradona was in contention for the No. 10 shirt as a striker on the left side of midfield, the position occupied at first by Valencia and later by Kempes. I'm not prepared to guess at what might have happened if the vote had gone to Maradona, but I must say he's the best I've seen.

He came from the back streets of Buenos Aires, the streets near the slaughter houses where his father worked in a bone-yard and raised eight children. By the time Maradona was nine, every football scout in Argentina knew of him, but he signed for shabby, unfashionable little Argentinos Juniors because that's where his best pal had gone.

He came on as a substitute for one of Menotti's representative teams when so small and young that the opposition thought he was the mascot! At fifteen, playing with full-grown men, his superiority was unmistakable. He has many qualities: intelligence, speed,

35

courage, strength, and a near perfect control of the ball. He reads a game better than anyone and can put a ball wherever he wishes with the nerve to attempt the impossible. He's not tall, yet few defenders dare feel confident about beating him in the air. He has the patience to work on improving his natural skills. For instance, I've seen him walk around for ages with a ball bouncing gently on his forehead. He'll keep it there for 1,000 bounces without difficulty.

Tranquillity returned after the decision about the final twenty-two. Nothing was allowed to disturb us and even the special visitors with permission to enter the camp would have to talk their way past a series of checkpoints manned by police and soldiers. The cordon protected us from being pestered by autograph hunters, ticket-seekers and those well-meaning optimists who unwittingly put pressure on teams by telling them how easily they'll win.

The tournament dawned with Argentina in the peak of physical condition, free from tension and completely relaxed. And then Hungary scored first in our opening match!

# 4 WORLD CUP 1978

Nerves are almost always the cause when golfers miss simple, short putts and when footballers blast penalties high or wide, or when whole teams freeze, as Argentina did against Hungary at the start of the 1978 World Cup. There is no defence against sporting nerves, even a perfect preparation is no defence – and ours had seemed perfect.

We had played fourteen warm-up matches, eight of them full international fixtures. Our months in camp had gone smoothly. We were at home. River Plate stadium in Buenos Aires was filled with 77,000 of our fans to welcome us with a blizzard of ticker-tape and there wasn't a Hungarian to be heard – if, indeed, they had any supporters present apart from a few members of their embassy staff. Not only was the nation behind us, but also the world's bookies.

Our opening group was anything but easy. Italy, Hungary, France and Argentina were all due to play each other once to decide which two teams would qualify for the second round. It was a closely matched group with apparently little to choose between the teams, yet the bookies made us odds on favourites to qualify with Italy; they also listed us as second favourites for the World Cup at 5–1 against (Brazil were the favourites at 5–2).

However, although everything seemed right, we were stiff with tension due to the expectations of the crowd and the importance of a match we dare not lose. The belief, based on a 5–1 friendly win a year earlier in 1977, that Hungary were easy to beat cramped our play. We couldn't get going and fell behind after only ten minutes.

The Hungarians marked man for man as we knew they would and also attacked with wingers. A thrust from both wings put them ahead when Nagy's shot from the left was parried by Fillol to Csapo who darted from the right to score a simple goal. Reeling from this shock, we gathered our strength and equalized within five minutes from a rehearsed free kick. Someone made a dummy run to distract the defenders; I passed the ball to Kempes and his shot was parried by the 'keeper. Luque pounced on the loose ball for an open goal.

In the eighty-fourth minute Gujdar, in Hungary's goal, again failed to grasp the ball and his error resulted in a winning goal for substitute Bertoni, as well as causing an explosive finish in which Hungary's two greatest stars were sent off. They were Tibor Nyilasi, a lanky midfielder, one of Europe's neatest one-touch players, and Andras Torocsik, a wonderful centre-forward who is unfortunately handicapped by a difficult temperament.

The dismissals virtually ended Hungary's hopes of qualifying because Nyilasi and Torocsik were barred from the next match but, as there had been continual Hungarian dissent and several criminal fouls from the moment we took command, I felt that the Portuguese referee had no option but to produce his red card.

After the match we felt exhausted, drained by the occasion and by our effort; yet, four days later, we had to spur ourselves into action again. France was our opponent and the French were amongst the most attractive players in the tournament. Their striker, Bernard Lacombe, had won a gold watch for scoring against Italy in only thirty-eight seconds (the first and fastest goal of the World Cup) but the French could not follow up their initial success and lost that opening match 2–1.

And 2–1 was also the score with which we won to put France out of the reckoning although a draw would have been a fairer reflection of a good, exciting game featuring three magnificent saves for us by Fillol. The French considered themselves unlucky when Didier Six missed an open goal in the second half. They were most unhappy about a first-half penalty against their stylish sweeper, Marius Trésor. No one denied that Trésor handled the ball in his fall but the argument raged over whether or not it was intentional; at any rate, Passarella scored from the penalty and, on the hour, Platini equalized for France.

A few minutes after France's goal we were the ones who began suffering from bad luck. We withdrew Valencia and sent on Alonso who was injured within minutes and Ortis was rushed on as a substitute for the substitute. Centre-forward Luque was also injured. This was serious for Argentina because his damaged elbow kept him out for two matches; fortunately, he scored the winning goal before the injury began to take its toll. I had a close-up view of the goal after running from midfield to give him the pass. I expected Luque to play a one-touch return; instead, he ran on and on while I fumed to myself: 'Pass it here. I'm in the clear, I've more chance than you.' At that moment, his shot hit the back of the net!

I was afraid that the French might claim offside against me, but they kept quiet and the linesman's flag stayed down. I am sure I was extremely close to an infringement.

Luque's goal sent us into the second round along with Italy who had beaten Hungary earlier in the day. That night the Ninth of July Avenue was choked for the first time by our celebrating fans. Four days later we lost 1–0 to Italy in the final match of the group but still the fans danced round the obelisk.

The Italians hadn't needed to beat us. A draw would have suited them equally well because their superior goal difference (5–2 against our 4–2) would have kept them above us in the group table. Anything but defeat would make them group winners with the privilege of remaining in Buenos Aires to play their three second-round matches at River Plate. Our chances of victory were slim. We were weakened by injuries, Luque and Alonso were out, Valencia was carrying a knock and I was under treatment. We made no scoring chances, they made only one when Bettega slid from the left to finish a clever combination with Paolo Rossi.

Next day we travelled some 200 miles to Rosario, a thriving river port with a skyline of grain elevators. It's no beauty spot but we were glad of the change. We weren't sorry to see the back of Buenos Aires for a while. The fanatical support at River Plate had lifted the opposition almost as much as it had helped us. It was due to a fault in the stadium's layout. River Plate, like Wembley, has a running track between the pitch and the stands so crowd noise is diffused. Rosario's ground was compact with 40,000 fans in two tiers almost on top of the pitch. They could support with maximum impact.

The composition of the Rosario group suited us. Four of the five surviving European teams (Italy, Holland, Austria and West Germany) were in the other group where we were happy to let them fight it out. Poland were the only Europeans in our group and we didn't regard them as a threat, not after our 3–1 win against the Poles in a recent friendly. Similarly, we discounted Peru, one of our two South American rivals in the group. We had beaten the Peruvians at home and away in our warm-up programme and we felt confident of winning again.

The remaining team, however, was Brazil. They were another matter: three times winners of the World Cup and unbeaten by us under Menotti's managership. 'Beat them now and the group's yours,' he said.

Luque was still missing when we met the Poles as his injury had been followed by his brother's death in a road crash. 'Cometh the hour, cometh the man' as the English say. The man was Mario Kempes. He scored twice.

These goals, his first of the series, started the run that earned him the 'Golden Boot'. It was always on the cards that Kempes would blossom in Rosario because the city teemed with fans who adored him as the star of Rosario Central before he was sold to Valencia in Spain.

Fillol again played superbly and saved a penalty from the Polish captain, Kasiu Deyna, who spent a couple of subsequent seasons at Manchester City. Deyna, a penalty expert, would be the first to concede that this one wasn't among his best; yet, on the other hand, any goalkeeper saving a World Cup penalty is entitled to feel pleased with himself.

Argentina 2, Poland 0 was my best performance; I ran through the defence before finding Kempes with a pass near the eighteen-yard line for his first goal. My pass to Bertoni began the build-up for the second goal. Ricky Villa made his World Cup début in this match, replacing Valencia in the forty-sixth minute as we gained gradual control.

The Poles think themselves unlucky to have been without their giant centre-half, Gorgon, and to have missed six scoring chances, apart from the penalty. I don't agree; I thought we outplayed Poland. They had no player to compare with Kempes and no defender able to hold him. From that day on, Kempes was our No. 1 player.

Brazil reached the same conclusion about the importance of Kempes. They decided to mark him closely in the next match. The chosen shadow was Chicão, a tall midfielder from São Paulo who had appeared twice, briefly, as a substitute. They prevented Kempes scoring but the match was the usual Brazil v. Argentina war. It is strange that two of the most skilful sides in the world always bring out the worst in each other.

Ricky Villa came on again (substituting for me in the forty-sixth minute) and made a name for himself immediately with two titanic tackles. Generally speaking, however, the match was bad and we were happy only about the scoreline. A draw (0–0 after a missed chance apiece) meant that both Argentina and Brazil retained a chance of reaching the final, depending on the results of our concluding fixtures.

The Brazilian team flew to Mendoza, 2,500 feet up in the foothills of the Andes. Their last game in the group was against Poland. They won 3–1 with a free kick by Nelinho and two goals by Roberto from rebounds.

It was an afternoon kick-off and we watched on T.V. growing more depressed with every goal. Brazil had set us a daunting target for our evening match against Peru. Unless we won by at least 4–0, we were out of the final.

I was injured, so my task in the squad was to cheer up the others. It wasn't easy and even Menotti didn't sound entirely convincing as he kept assuring the team: 'Our fate is in our own hands now. We know exactly what we have to do – and you can do it.'

I sat at the touchline with Menotti, matching him cigarette for cigarette. My nerves were in shreds and their condition was not improved when, at the start, Oblitas, Peru's No. 11, hit our post. Peru let a second clear chance go begging before Kempes shot us ahead. His goal signalled the start of a non-stop onslaught and F.I.F.A. recorded fifteen direct scoring attempts by Argentina in the first half, but apart from the Kempes goal it seemed that nothing would go in. And then, in the forty-third minute, Tarantini scored with a header. It was the vital goal and, as so often happens, unplanned. Tarantini had never been known for his heading. What's more, he shouldn't even have been in Peru's penalty area. His job was to stay back.

Peru gave up in the second half. Their attitude was not unlike Hungary's in the World Cup qualifying match against England at Wembley in 1981. They showed no desire to exert themselves when the result was of no importance. A free kick by Kempes, two goals by Luque and one by Houseman finished them off: we won 6–0 and reached the final on a comfortable goal difference of eight for, none against, compared with Brazil's six for, one against.

The Brazilian reaction was disgraceful. Immediately after the match, their journalists and hordes of radio reporters began to spread rumours that Peru had been bribed to lose. Suspicion was thrown on Peru's goalkeeper, Ramón Quiroga, because he had been born in Argentina. Poor Quiroga! He was driven to issuing an open letter defending himself and his team-mates. Some Argentinian news-papers countered with the claim that wealthy Brazilian fans had offered the Peruvian players a special bonus to beat us; such a pay-ment, of course, would have been in complete breach of the World Cup rules. The Brazilian media brushed the charge aside while some of their sportswriters continued to profess inside knowledge of a bribe. Their allegation remained unsupported and, as any neutral spectator would confirm, untrue.

Some of the blame for these wild stories must rest on the late Claudio Coutinho, Brazil's team manager. Coutinho was fluent in four languages and courteous in all of them, except when losing! And his disappointment at failing to reach the final was not alleviated by the news that fans back home in Rio de Janeiro were burning his effigy in the streets. Coutinho had a duty to quash the rumours by making plain his disbelief in them; instead, he did nothing. Even worse, he fanned the flames by damning the Peruvian team, saying: 'They'll feel no pride when they next hear their anthem.'

Whatever the Brazilians liked to think, they could not alter the fact that we were in the World Cup final against Holland while they had to be content with the comparative crumb of playing for third place against Italy.

Argentina's entire population was beside itself with joy and excite-ment. Only one man among the 26,000,000 was sunk in gloom – and that was me. I had seen how splendidly Omar Larrosa had played as my stand-in against Peru and, in the closely guarded privacy of our camp at José Paz outside Buenos Aires, I worried over the very real risk of not being selected for the most important match of my life. There was a genuine case for preferring Larrosa. To put it briefly, he was on form and I was unfit, and the argument for continuing with the eleven who slaughtered Peru might have swayed any manager less loyal than Menotti.

One of Menotti's best kept secrets was that I'd been playing with a broken toe. It happened against France although there was no discomfort at the time. However, I felt a sharp pain in my left foot on the following morning and an X-ray revealed a fracture of the fourth toe.

From that day I was unable to train normally with the others and could play only with two injections, one on either side of the toe. This resulted in a loss of sensitivity in my foot and, as painkillers usually wear off after an hour, an unpleasant end to a game. Furthermore, trying to protect my left foot (or carry it, as players say) I twisted my right ankle in a run against Brazil. It was so bad I couldn't walk the 100 yards from our hotel to the training ground in Rosario and Kempes had to give me a piggyback. Continual injections had made the toe more sore than ever while the swollen right ankle needed heavy strapping. Yet Menotti brushed my fears aside, saying: 'You are going to play. You'll be O.K. with just a little injection and some bandages.'

I passed a fitness test of sorts but was under no illusions about the reason for my selection. Menotti picked me out of loyalty and in recognition of my services over the years. I'll never cease to be grateful. He knew he was sending out a wreck, a player with two bad ankles. I hadn't trained for three weeks and couldn't possibly last ninety minutes. I was O.K. for a World Cup final but not for any lesser match – and if I needed a lot of treatment afterwards, what did it matter?

We were all nervous about the final, but not as much as we had been before the Hungary match. Just reaching the final was a satisfactory achievement and, although we thought we could win it, victory was not of absolute importance. Menotti echoed this feeling in his team-talk. He stressed the need for fair play, saying: 'I want good behaviour. No play-acting. If you're knocked down but not hurt, get up and get on with the game. We're here to put on a show because the whole world is watching.'

It was unjust of European observers to accuse us of two acts of gamesmanship before the kick off. They claimed we arrived five minutes late on the pitch deliberately, but that wasn't so. The explanation was a mix-up by the stewards in the tunnel; no one seemed to be in charge and every order was countermanded. We shuffled our feet for what seemed like an age as the men with the walkie-talkies kept changing their minds . . . 'Come out. No, wait, a moment. It's all right now. One moment, just a moment please.'

Finally, as we lined up with the Dutch, I found myself alongside Rene van der Kerkhof and saw, as we exchanged pennants, that his

*Inside Argentina's dressing-room after the 6–0 victory against Peru that put us in the World Cup final. Centre-forward Leopoldo Luque shows off his underpants on the right, Passarella's arms hang round my shoulders in the centre, and Larrosa smiles across the treatment table in the foreground*

right forearm was covered in a heavy plaster. I went to Passarella, saying: 'He can't play with that, it's thick enough to break someone's jaw in a collision.' Menotti was called in; he protested to the Italian referee, Gonella, and a full-scale argument ensued.

The Dutch were furious over what they saw as attempted vitimization. The plaster had been worn in five preceding matches and they suspected us of saving up a complaint until it could cause maximum disruption. Johan Neeskens, who had learned Spanish with F.C. Barcelona, shouted: 'If that's how you want it, you can play the final on your own. We're off.'

His team-mates seemed ready to go with him and for a moment it looked as if there would be no World Cup final, at best, a long delay while the Dutch returned to their dressing-room for a second warm-up.

In retrospect, I regard the incident as a fuss over nothing. My objection to the plaster was completely justified, it was dangerous and in their hearts the Dutch knew we were right. They were angry about the timing of our complaint and pointed out that we should have raised the question earlier. However, we didn't know that the thing on Rene van der Kerkhof's forearm wasn't the light, protective covering permitted in the rules instead of a substantial plaster that could do as much damage as a knuckle-duster. The referee agreed with us and ruled that Rene must wrap his arm in a soft bandage.

The match began with a crude foul by a Dutch defender, Poortvliet, and I think many people interpreted it as a reaction to the argument before the kick-off. My opinion is different: I believe the Dutch had aggression on their minds long before then. They wore threatening expressions from the moment we arrived on the pitch; even our flags of friendship were greeted with glowering looks!

The noise from our 77,000 supporters streaming their giant banners down the terraces underlined Dutch captain Rudi Krol's remark: 'We're playing a nation, not a team.' Yet, there's no denying that Holland made a good job of it at the start. They created three early chances to score with a header by Rep that was just wide, a shot by Rensenbrink that Fillol somehow saved with his legs, and a drive by Rep that Fillol tipped over the bar. Then we scored in the thirty-eighth minute. Someone fouled me on the left and I started falling but managed to keep control. I touched the ball to Luque and his pass sent Kempes racing past Krol to beat the 'keeper.

My ankles began aching badly in the second half and I was afraid we might lose control of the midfield, so I went off in the sixty-fifth minute and Larrosa came on. The Dutch needed more power in the centre of their attack and had already made a substitution; they sent on Nanninga who headed an equalizer in the eighty-second minute. And then, in what must have been the closing seconds of injury time, the World Cup seemed to have been snatched away from us. Rensenbrink shot from a few yards out. I thought the ball was going in; it seemed impossible that the shot could stay out, but it hit the post and bounced away to safety.

There is no more convincing explanation for Rensenbrink's miss than the belief of our supporters that it was a triumph for prayer and willpower as twenty-six million Argentinians cried in unison: 'Ball out, ball out!'

So, as at Wembley in 1966, the World Cup final went into extra time. The additional half-hour proved too much for Holland whose energy had been used up in fighting to level the scores. We finished as the fitter side and won 3–1 with goals by Kempes and Bertoni.

The cup, that golden orange, was held aloft by Passarella and the terraces went crazy with delight. It was weeks later that I began wondering how many of the fans who idolized us as world champions had been the critics of Menotti's team-building.

I remember the horror of once picking up the popular *Goles* magazine and finding my face on the front cover defaced with a cross over the caption: 'Ardiles can't play.' Jorge Carrascosa, one of my clubmates at Huracán, was another prime target for *Goles* as the captain of Argentina. Carrascosa was only in his late twenties and still in his prime but he was weary of criticism and wanted more time with his family; he resigned the captaincy a couple of years before the 1978 World Cup and dropped out of international football.

The magazine admired Juan Carlos Lorenzo, the high priest of physical football who was then coaching Boca Juniors. It was anti-Menotti and the players closest to him, such as myself, Ricky Villa and Carrascosa.

Passarella, the centre-half and new skipper, was one of only three players enjoying mass support during Menotti's early days; the others were the goalkeeper, Fillol, and the winger, Bertoni, and I would guess that Luque and Tarantini had more admirers than critics. The rest of us were under a continual hammering from the media and the crowd.

The fans wanted me to be replaced by Juan José López, a star of River Plate. He was so famous that everyone referred to him by his initials J.J. He was slightly older than I – twenty-seven to my twenty-five at the time that Menotti was putting the final touches to his side.

J.J. represented a serious threat to me because he is a wonderful player. But he had made the mistake of clashing with Menotti and resigning from the national team. It was the old 'club v. country' argument; J.J. was more interested in pursuing honours with River Plate than in spending months under special training with Argentina. 'Right,' said Menotti, 'that's the end of you' – and he stuck by his decision despite a campaign for J.J.'s reinstatement. Menotti relented only to the extent of including J.J. in his final forty.

The shadow of J.J. loomed over me until we won the World Cup. Even then there were still River Plate supporters prepared to argue that the 1978 team would have been stronger with him in my place. In fact, we were not interchangeable; J.J.'s forte was attack but he didn't cover defensive ground as I did and Menotti wanted a balancing player, someone able to combine both functions.

In 1982, J.J. was transferred to Talleres (Córdoba) following a quarrel with Alfredo di Stefano who had taken over as manager of the River Plate club. It seemed that at thirty-one he was starting to fade from international reckoning with the result that my name would no longer be the signal for derisive whistling by López fans.

It's awful when supporters turn against a player. We feel stripped of confidence, clumsy and unable to do anything right. Things were so bad that, after a goal-less draw against Uruguay in which I had been the butt of the crowd's tension, I told Passarella and Ricky Villa (he was getting harsh treatment, too): 'I'm quitting the squad, I just can't take any more of this barracking.'

They tried to reassure me, saying: 'Don't be silly, you're going to be all right.' Sure enough, my form began to return. I played well in an untelevized provincial match that Menotti's team won 5–1, but I still needed to convince the public when the cameras were on me.

That opportunity came during two friendly matches against Peru. We won both matches. I played well, but that wasn't all. An incident in the second game swung the crowd to my cause: Oblitas of Peru moved in fast, attempting to close me down; I countered with a dummy, then shoved the ball between his legs. That's what spectators love in Argentina. At last, I was a star.

48

# 5 ENGLAND

I had six free days at home before flying to London for the medical examinations required by Tottenham Hotspur and the Football League. It was just long enough for doubts to set in.

Educated Argentinians loved the idea of life in England but the country was uncharted territory for Argentinian footballers, so I had no advice or experience to draw on. I wondered what to expect and worried about the risk of a hostile reception because of the strained relations between the British and Argentinian governments.

At that time, the summer of 1978, Argentina had no ambassador in London and there was no end to the controversy over our claim to the Falkland Islands. We call them the Malvinas and are taught from infancy to regard them as part of our country, stolen by the British in 1832. No one foresaw then the coming to power of General Galtieri who, as the new military president of Argentina, would seize this diplomatic bull by the horns and invade the islands in 1982. As I flew home to start training for the World Cup in Spain, a British battle fleet was preparing to sail 8,000 miles south to recapture them.

The Malvinas, or Falklands, seemed less of a flashpoint in 1978 than Britain's role as boundary adjudicator in a long-standing dispute between Argentina and Chile over the Beagle Channel at the southernmost tip of South America. The channel joins the Atlantic Ocean to the Pacific and by ruling that three small islands in it belonged to Chile Britain interfered seriously with what we regarded as our lawful frontier. We blamed the Queen because the judgment, although the work of functionaries, was handed down in her name.

War with Chile seemed the only recourse and there were several skirmishes in 1980 before the intervention of the Pope, as mediator, prevented the outbreak of full hostilities.

Our football fans also nursed a grievance against England; they had never forgiven Sir Alf Ramsey, the former England manager, for saying, after his team's 1–0 victory in the quarter-finals of the 1966 World Cup, that, 'Argentina played like animals.'

Ramsey, the Falklands and the Beagle combined as causes of the ill feeling in Buenos Aires towards England's 1977 tour team under Don Revie. Their match against Argentina at Boca Juniors' ground was supposedly a friendly but the crowd barracked the British national anthem, shouted insults, waved anti-British banners and made it plain that the English weren't welcome.

Would English supporters retaliate against myself and Ricky Villa? No one seemed to know. Some of my friends warned: 'You're bound to have trouble,' while others thought: 'A year is a long time, so it'll have been forgotten in England; also no one there will have heard of the Beagle Channel. You'll be all right.'

Reports in Argentinian newspapers added to the confusion. English fans seemed to want us, but the players' representatives didn't. Cliff Lloyd, secretary of the Professional Footballers Association, threatened: 'If Ardiles and Villa are granted work permits, we would probably object in order to protect the interests of our members. These players are from outside the Commonwealth and the European Economic Community and, as far as I'm aware, there are no opportunities for British players in Argentina.'

Ron Greenwood, England's manager, took the opposite view, saying: 'The prospect of Ardiles and Villa playing here would give the new season a tremendous boost. Villa is big and strong and looks the type who could do well in the English game while Ardiles is the best right-sided midfield player in the World Cup, and he's very similar to Alan Ball. I certainly don't believe that imported players would harm the game. That hasn't been the case in cricket.'

The Professional Footballers then countered with a statement by Gordon Taylor, a former chairman who is now their full-time secretary, in which he said: 'We have asked for clarification from the Department of Employment on whether they are satisfied that Spurs tried to sign players of similar quality to Ardiles and Villa in England.

'We have been criticized for our attitude in this situation but we represent the interests of English players in a contracting industry and if the trickle of foreign players becomes a flow it would be detrimental to our members. Whichever way you look at it, there could already be two English players out of jobs at Spurs.

'There is also the wider issue of the possible effect on English football. Cricket has shown that too many foreign imports impede the development of our own younger players.

'We feel it is right to make our views known at the outset. There's no point in taking a stand when there are twenty foreign players, rather than just two.'

Our names even figured in questions in the House of Commons: John Grant, the Employment Under-Secretary, said: 'In the light of replies from the Football Association, the Football League and the P.F.A., a decision will be taken a soon as possible as to whether the applications on behalf of Ardiles and Villa satisfy the criteria of the work permit scheme. This is normal procedure, the same thing happens in the case of entertainers and musicians.'

Osvaldo de Santis, the president of Huracán, revealed that the actual fee received for me was £205,000 and that Racing received the same for Ricky Villa. Extras in the shape of tax, signing-on fees and a levy by the Argentinian F.A. had raised Tottenham's total outlay to £555,000. Another row then broke out over whether any of that money, in contravention of F.I.F.A. and League rules had been paid to an agent.

Disputes over one issue or another dragged on for nearly three weeks before the League's management committee met in London and pronounced themselves finally satisfied with the transfers. We were cleared to make our débuts at Nottingham Forest in the opening League game of the season.

While the various official bodies argued, Ricky and I paid a flying visit to London for medical examinations. We made the welcome discovery that England, far from being hostile, was full of friendly fans. We met a group of them at Heathrow and I even remember the names of two of them: Glen McBride and Graham Carpenter who, because our plane had been delayed by a strike in Madrid, had to wait sixteen hours to greet us but said: 'We'd do it all over again just to show how much it means to have Ardiles and Villa here.'

Other fans expressed their admiration in hard cash. They backed us to win the League championship for Tottenham. The odds plummeted from 66–1 to 25–1 against but, as results soon proved, it wasn't a good bet.

We landed around midnight, tired after twenty-eight hours of continual travel, including eight hours delay in the transit lounge at Madrid, yet still in surprisingly good heart. I had started to see the move to England through my wife's eyes. Always spirited and optimistic, she regarded Tottenham as a great challenge whose non-acceptance could cause only lasting regret. It's the attitude illustrated in the English expression: 'Nothing ventured, nothing gained.' My hopes were high when Keith Burkinshaw stepped forward to meet us as we came through Customs.

Our subsequent drive puzzled me. I had expected some signs of a big city with perhaps a glimpse of Buckingham Palace or Nelson's Column; instead, I saw only small factories and residential areas. Now, as an honorary Londoner, I know the reason. Keith was taking us to a hotel used by the England team and had gone round the outskirts.

Every inch of me was examined by doctors next morning. Bits they couldn't reach were X-rayed, yet to my great relief, they missed the only part that wouldn't have withstood scrutiny: my chipped toe.

A doctor in Argentina had told me the injury would heal itself without requiring plaster but I worried in case my signing was ruled out by English doctors taking a different view, so I kept quiet when I noticed that the X-rays of my feet showed only the insteps and ankles.

Another clue to my injury was missed by both supporters and the media that afternoon at the ground. Everyone had pictures of me shaking hands on the terraces, strolling on the pitch and talking to my new team-mates but none of me kicking a ball. Without making it obvious, I stayed clear of action pictures because I could neither shoot nor run. My foot was as bad as that, and it nagged for a further two months until it cleared up without treatment, as the doctor in Buenos Aires had forecast.

I told the press conference: 'The thick green grass at Tottenham is a surprise and makes me feel like playing.' It didn't seem polite to mention that White Hart Lane itself was something of a disappointment, old-fashioned compared with Huracán or Ricky's modern ground at Racing; I kept my opinion to myself and the charm of the ground grew on me until now, with the opening of a £4,500,000 stand in 1982, no one can accuse the club of being behind the times.

*Tottenham, here we are! With Ricky Villa on our first day in London. The famous old stand in the background was replaced in 1982 by a modern two-tier stand costing £4,500,000*

We had a free hour before flying home next day and decided to spend it in Oxford Street so we could tell our families that we had seen something of the London glamour awaiting them. Little did we know then that we would be living no nearer to the West End than Chigwell, a nice Essex suburb but undeniably quiet in comparison with downtown Buenos Aires, a city that does even less sleeping than London.

The club had found a house for us in Chigwell; it was waiting when Ricky and I returned from Argentina in early August and served as a base while we looked around for permanent accommodation. Chigwell, being on the Underground's Central Line, is handy for shopping trips into London but hasn't much in the way of leisure activities for foreign footballers. We found nothing to do apart from visiting restaurants although, to be fair, we would have been handicapped anywhere until we had picked up more of the language.

I couldn't understand the theatre, the cinema or T.V. apart from sports programmes, and, despite seven years of studying English at school and university, I had to read newspapers slowly in order to grasp the full meaning of stories. Many headline words – 'Sack', for example – baffled me. My wife had stayed in Argentina with my elder son, Pablo, while awaiting the birth of Federico; her absence added loneliness to the difficulties of adjusting to life in a strange land.

I declined the club's offer to put me up in a hotel; instead, I accepted Ricky's kind invitation to continue staying with him and his family in Chigwell but, even with them for company, my thoughts kept straying to Buenos Aires.

I was always reaching for the 'phone, telling myself: 'It's not easy for Sylvia to call England. She'll have to go through the international operator and maybe wait a couple of hours for a line, while I can dial direct.' I started phoning home daily, sometimes as often as three times a day. The habit was cured by the very first phone bill; I'd been spending an average of nearly £200 a week!

A chauffeur-driven car was offered by the club and that, too, was declined because Ricky and I wanted to do our own motoring. We persuaded the club, justifiably worried about our safety, that London traffic presented no problems to men accustomed to whizzing around Buenos Aires where every driver believes himself to be Carlos Reutemann.

We bought a big map but what we really needed was a point of reference, an idea of the relationship of one place to another. In our early excursions, we would turn right or left without really knowing where we were going or how to get back. However, we could read signs – and when it suited us we couldn't read the signs quite as well. Oxford Street is a case in point. There's no left turn into it from Charing Cross Road; we turned left, though, and no one stopped us. From then on, we always turned left until we realized it was forbidden.

My nearside front wheel scraped a lot of kerbs before I got the hang of driving on the left. Roundabouts were another menace. I was forever reminding myself not to take them anti-clockwise as most of the rest of the world does. However, my confidence grew until I had no qualms about navigating English roads – and then came the affair of dinner with the diplomats.

Argentina's consul had invited Ricky and myself to dine at his home, also offering to send a car for us.

'It's not necessary,' I said, thanking him. 'I'll drive us over.'

'You'll never find it.'

'Yes, we will. It's near Harrods.' I neglected to mention that I'd never driven through London as far as Knightsbridge.

Doubts set in somewhere near Oxford Circus when I asked for directions from a passer-by, who gave them willingly but too quickly. A motorist, perhaps recognizing us or struck by our baffled expressions, came to the rescue, saying: 'Follow me as far as Hyde Park' – but once in the park with our guide gone I couldn't see a sign for Harrods.

A parked police car was my next hope and I asked for directions, unaware of my tendency to swallow English word-endings. 'Follow us,' they said.

'No problem. We've got a police escort,' I told Ricky and sped out of the park behind them and away down a long, busy road before they signalled to us: 'Keep straight on.'

We did, for mile after mile, until occasional fields began appearing.

'Something's wrong here,' I said, then almost immediately saw the sign explaining it. Not Harrods, but Harrow.

Someone compared us later to those bewildered North American tourists who, it was said, kept arriving at Tooting Common after requesting directions to an exhibition of the Egyptian treasures of Tutankhamun.

Now I make my requests explicit and ask for 'Harrods shop'. Happily, the mix-up didn't cost us dinner although we had to pay a taxi to lead us back, rather late, to the consul's house.

I hadn't been to Harrods before but it seemed familiar because Buenos Aires had a store of the same name, although it's tiny compared with the London emporium. Argentinian shops are mostly small, boutiques almost, so my first impression of England was of the huge shops and the honesty of the customers in them; I know that shop-lifting goes on but it seems negligible, considering the temptations. It wasn't only their honesty that was striking about the English, but their gentleness, their eagerness to help a stranger and their forbearance as I mangled their language. 'Please', 'yes', 'no', 'thank you', 'very nice' was about the extent of my vocabulary in the first few weeks – terrible considering I'd had seven years of lessons. I knew more words, of course, but couldn't summon up the nerve to use them. All my English teachers in Argentina, I realized, had spoken too much Spanish at the expense of conversational practice.

Speaking is the hardest thing for a foreigner in England; the next hardest is listening and understanding English spoken at a speed never before encountered in South American classrooms. Grammar was the next hurdle, the knack of stringing words together. Until what I'd been taught began coming back, I could frame only single-word questions, such as 'Ground?' or 'Cheshunt?' when inquiring about venues for training.

I could say 'salt', 'pepper' and 'knife' at the team's meals, knowing there would be laughter if either Ricky or I asked for a knife when meaning a spoon. Today, even after years of hearing it, the dressing-room still chuckles when I ask for 'chin pads'. The laughter, though, was always kind and good-humoured. Tottenham's players couldn't have been more helpful and I'll always remember with particular affection two who've left the club: Peter Taylor and John Pratt. Peter has a lively mind and was given special responsibility for us when we joined the team. I called him 'my manager' and flourished an English-Spanish dictionary at him; he went out immediately to buy one for himself and our early conversations were hilariously slow with much thumbing of pages. Peter's kindness extended far beyond the ground and, in the months when I was on my own, he took me to his home and introduced me to many of his friends.

I met John Pratt when Ricky and I joined the team on their pre-season tour; they were staying at Zeist, the Dutch F.A.'s training camp where the many amenities include snooker and table tennis. Someone, I can't remember who, asked out of politeness if Ricky might like a frame, never guessing that Ricky is a star with the cue. It

*My new team-mates wondered if I could play table tennis. 'A little,' I said, not showing them this action picture from the days when I was the under-eighteen champion of Córdoba*

was comical to see the exchange of glances among the Tottenham lads when Ricky won. 'Hey, what's the game?' they must have been thinking, unaware that snooker (like football, rugby and cricket) is among the British imports to Argentina.

I shrugged disarmingly when the players turned to me, wondering if I'd ever handled a table-tennis bat. 'A little,' I said, not wishing to boast of having been under-eighteen champion of Córdoba and still in regular practice. John Pratt, the team's table-tennis king, was offered as an opponent and kidded along as we knocked up: 'I'll kill him. One each for England.' Poor John, such a nice fellow and so disappointed when I beat him easily.

A couple of days later Ricky and I made our débuts for Tottenham in a 3–1 victory at Royal Antwerp in Belgium; Ian Moores scored with two headers and Glenn Hoddle with a penalty. And then, after further friendlies in Holland and in Dublin, it was straight into the First Division. It was a lot harder than table tennis.

# 6 FAILURE AND SUCCESS

Ricky Villa and I were not the only Argentinians imported into English football after the 1978 World Cup. Three others signed, but their stories had unhappy endings.

Alberto Tarantini played with me in the World Cup final. He was our left-back and ever-present in the competition, but he was a failure at Birmingham City.

Claudio Marangoni was an Argentinian version of Trevor Brooking, but Sunderland cancelled his contract after only a year.

Alex Sabella was a hot prospect at the River Plate club, but he suffered relegation and rejection in England.

Their stories ought to be a warning to managers of the many risks involved in signing foreign footballers because each of the three failed for a different reason, none more surprisingly than Marangoni. He seemed heaven-sent for England, being fluent in the language, and his wife, a former air hostess of British descent, also spoke good English. They both wanted to come and, except for lack of pace, there was no question about Marangoni's ability as a player. He was two-footed, a strong tackler, good in the air, a free-kick specialist and with a mental speed that compensated for any slowness over the ground. Also, at six feet one inch and thirteen stone, he was big enough to look after himself in the physical battles.

Sunderland paid their record fee of £320,000 to San Lorenzo for Marangoni midway through their promotion season of 1979-80. It looked like a bargain, and I couldn't imagine him not being successful. What went wrong? 'The manager won't give me a chance to

*Alex Sabella, the first Argentinian to play for two clubs in the English League –*
*Sheffield United and Leeds United*

play my way,' said Marangoni when I asked him. 'He's always wanting more running, more physical output.'

As I've mentioned, running was the only thing he couldn't do. I've often wondered if Sunderland ever regret getting only twenty games in a year from an all-purpose midfielder who could win the ball, pass the ball and, if necessary do the sweeping. When I last heard of him, Marangoni was back in Argentina playing superbly for my old club, Huracán. The manager, Ken Knighton, also left Sunderland in the same season and was out of work for six months before taking over at Orient.

Sabella was signed by Sheffield United for a fee that was quoted at various figures between £80,000 and £160,000. The deal went through at the same time as my own transfer. The signing manager was Harry Haslam, who had been responsible for tipping off Tottenham about the availability of Ricky Villa and myself. 'Happy Harry' made a handsome profit for his club whatever the fee. In April 1980 he sold Sabella to Leeds United for £400,000.

Sabella is the only Argentinian to have played for two clubs in the English League, but he has had a hard time at both of them. Sheffield United were relegated to the Third Division in his first season – and he took that badly. Leeds were also struggling when he joined them and then Jimmy Adamson, the manager who signed Sabella, was sacked six months later.

Fans like Sabella's wonderful little touches on the ball but a foreigner hoping to make an impression in the English game also needs an appetite for hard work. Alex hasn't got that. So Leeds lost a lot of money in January 1982 when they sold him to the Buenos Aires club, Estudiantes de la Plata, for only £70,000.

Tarantini, the third unsuccessful transfer, would always be in my team. He's a winner, but trying to stop Birmingham from toppling into the Second Division was the wrong job for him. He didn't have an outstanding World Cup, even though ever-present throughout the seven matches; I think he was distracted by outside worries, principally a quarrel over his contract with Boca Juniors. He left Boca and was going to join New York Cosmos, then Barcelona came in. Signings were announced, then suddenly cancelled. September arrived with Tarantini still a free agent but without a club. I mean no disrespect to Birmingham in saying that they then became his last resort. He was desperate to sign for somebody and had nowhere else to go, but it was a case of the wrong man for the wrong club.

Tarantini, with his fierce hunger for medals, was a player for glory-hunting teams, not for middle-of-the-table teams and still less for a club that had won nothing in its entire history.

Birmingham's manager, Jim Smith, seemed to fall into the trap of assuming that a South American origin is a guarantee of exceptional skill; in fact, Tarantini has only average skills. Unhappily, he tried to fulfil expectations by attempting things beyond his capabilities. He'd never been a midfielder in Argentina but he played in the midfield against Tottenham and, as I expected, made a few horrible mistakes. It was a transfer that never had a chance. Birmingham were already at the bottom when he arrived, so he played all his games in a struggling side and then, after six months, they sold their only forward star, Trevor Francis. How could Tarantini be at his best in such circumstances? However, failure with Birmingham doesn't mean that Tarantini wouldn't have succeeded elsewhere in England. With Manchester United he could have been sensational. The presence of big-name team-mates would have roused him and, at the same time, removed the pressure of trying to be a club's saviour from the impossible position of left back. Full-backs can't improve sides on their own. That's done by signing a striker or a midfielder or, in certain cases a goalkeeper or central defender. I wouldn't pay big money for a full-back; it's not a key position but one that should be filled by promoting reserves and juniors. So importing a foreign defender was another basic flaw in the Tarantini transfer.

I would always pick Tarantini, average though he is, because he is capable of aggressive tackling and has courage and determination, which outweigh the flaws of his moderate heading, his inability to beat a man with the ball, and his tendency towards inaccurate passing.

I feel that Tarantini has proved my case by the success of his return to Argentina where, under the guidance of Alfredo di Stefano, he not only helped River Plate win the championship but was also voted their Footballer of the Year.

Many players become big names on no more than Tarantini's natural skills. I'd choose Steve Coppell as an example. He's neither creative, nor particularly skilful or good in the air, but he is strong and honest. He works hard, runs a lot and is highly intelligent. Intelligence is the main quality I seek in assessing a player. Coppell, despite only average talent, plays regularly for England.

I won't spare myself the same tests, for I'm not unlike Coppell. A scouting report on me might read: 'Hopeless in the air. No left foot, inconsistent with long passes and only reasonably skilful.' With such drawbacks, how did I ever get a place in the World Cup? Without wishing to sound boastful, I'd say largely because of good vision. I read situations quickly and from that comes my creativity.

Anyway, Tarantini, Marangoni and Sabella are in the record books as Argentinians who, for a variety of reasons, failed in England. On the first Saturday of September 1978, two more names seemed certain to be added to their number – those of Osvaldo Ardiles and Ricky Villa. It was the afternoon when Liverpool thrashed us 7–0 at Anfield, the lowest point of my football career so far. Four days later we were beaten 3–1 at home by Swansea and knocked out of the League Cup. Swansea were only a Third Division club and those defeats meant that our competitive record in England was disastrous: played six, won none.

A glossary of Spanish-English football phrases had been published by the *Sunday Mirror* when we signed, one of them being: '*Estoy así enfermo como un papagayo*, which is, literally, 'I'm as sick as a parrot' and although the expression is not current in Argentina, I knew the feeling exactly.

Keith Burkinshaw was being compelled to modify his early optimism. He'd been saying in July: 'We've got to work on raising basic skills in England; until we do, we can't compete at the highest level. I'm hoping some of the skill of Ardiles and Villa will rub off and lift the level of the team.' Now he was warning: 'Rome wasn't built in a day. It will take time for the Argentinian players to fit in.'

A crowd survey showed that Tottenham were the biggest attraction away from home with average attendances at our away games of 37,269, which was far ahead (by nearly 6,000 a match) of Manchester United, who traditionally top this kind of table. But the League table on the morning of the second Saturday of September 1978 showed us as second from bottom with only two points. 'When all is said and done,' I said to Ricky sardonically, 'the Second Division in England is not all that bad.'

Yet the future had seemed full of bright promise only a month previously when we drew at Nottingham Forest in our first League game of the season. I knew so little of English football in those days! I was unaware that Forest were the League champions and I'd never heard of Brian Clough. But when I heard our players talking with

*Team-mates in Argentina but opponents in England – myself and Alberto Tarantini reunited after his debut in October 1978 for Birmingham City, but his stay in England was short and unsuccessful*

deep respect of the opposition and their manager, I realized that the fixture list hadn't given us an easy start and yet, although I was usually nervous before matches, I was calm at Nottingham.

The kick-off was delayed for a quarter of an hour while hooligans fought on the pitch, but I wasn't upset by the delay. I put on all my kit except a shirt, draped a towel over my shoulders and stood in front of the dressing-room mirror combing my hair, dabbing it with water, then combing it again. What else could I do? I couldn't talk properly to my team-mates and I couldn't understand the manager's last-minute instructions. They were too fast for me. Keith used an interpreter to give us private briefings on tactics but I learned better from his blackboard diagrams.

There was a story of Keith starting one of these team-talks by making a globe sign with his hands while saying 'Ball', then another sign for crossbar and posts while saying 'Goal'.

I was supposed to have objected: 'But, boss, Ricky and I know these words.'

To which he replied: 'This isn't for you, I'm talking to the others.'

It was a joke that went the rounds when we started losing. No one dreamt of telling it after we'd taken a point from Forest; instead they went home talking about Ricky's cool equalizer in the twenty-fifth minute.

We'd fallen behind when a cross from the Scotland winger John Robertson wasn't cut out and left Martin O'Neill with two shooting chances. The first was blocked, but the second went in.

John Gorman, whose career ended prematurely through injury, began the move leading to our equalizer. He freed Ian Moores on the left, Moores crossed so suddenly that Ricky was left one-against-one with Peter Shilton. The big goalkeeper flew out – and he looks as big as a lorry when doing that – but Ricky dummied him. As Shilton went down, Ricky swayed left and scored. It was 1–1.

If Ricky were always as calm, he'd score a lot more goals; he's two-footed and powerful but over-anxiety is his undoing in the penalty area. By trying to make absolutely certain, he loses his chance.

White Hart Lane turned into a passable imitation of River Plate stadium on the following Wednesday evening for our home début. Every telephone directory in North London must have been shredded for a ticker-tape welcome from 48,000 spectators. We ran out in a paper blizzard to kick off against Aston Villa but the joy

66

was short-lived. Villa beat us 4–1. I've tried to put this calamity out of my mind; I never see much profit in mulling over defeats. Just for the record, though, Villa's scorers were Allan Evans, John Gregory, Brian Little and Gary Shelton. Our goal was a penalty by Glenn Hoddle for a foul against me.

Keith told the press conference: 'I'm disappointed for the fans who expected great things, but Aston Villa denied us space more than any side we've met for a season. Now we've got to learn from this setback.'

A 2–2 draw with Chelsea in the next match was a slight improvement. Ricky and I figured in both goals. His back-heel and my pass made the first goal for John Duncan; for the second, I beat two men in the box and then Ricky pulled the ball back to let Gerry Armstrong score. Ominously, each goal was followed immediately by equalizers from Kenny Swain. The Tottenham team was a defenders' nightmare but our failings in that department were overlooked on this occasion because nearly everyone was talking instead about Ricky brushing aside a full challenge from 'Chopper' Ron Harris.

'He went straight through the tackle,' said Chelsea's manager, Ken Shellito, incredulously.

Neither Ricky nor I had heard of 'Chopper' Harris but it seemed he was London's senior hard man and not to be treated disdainfully. The incident reinforced Ricky's reputation as a mighty man; in training, no one would contest a fifty-fifty ball with him, remembering only too vividly his devastating World Cup tackle on Batista of Brazil.

I was quietly amused by the way everyone avoided trouble with Ricky; I knew he was a nice guy, not at all violent, and that his scything of Batista's thigh was quite unintentional.

Immediately after 'Chopper' Harris we ran into Tommy Smith. I'd never heard of Smith either, even though he had captained Liverpool and rejoiced in the nickname of 'Anfield Iron'. But I learnt all about him after only a minute of our League Cup tie at Swansea, who were then in the Third Division.

Smith wore No. 4 for them, and their manager, John Toshack, had been saying earlier: 'Ardiles and Villa looked good against Chelsea last Saturday but Chelsea didn't have Tommy Smith in

*Following pages: Our first League game for Tottenham – Ricky Villa is on the left, I have the ball after escaping from Peter Withe of Nottingham Forest*

their side. His experience and determination will help make all the difference.'

How much experience does it require to commit a nasty, late tackle? I'd received a ball in midfield, paused to weigh up the options and then delivered a pass. The next thing I knew was Smith's boot hitting me high on the left thigh. I'm so light and nimble that it's difficult to catch me with a fair tackle, or even with an unfair one if I'm expecting it. I just wasn't ready for a sly trick like Smith's; I was angry with him and with the referee, who didn't even take his name. Treatment with a pain-killing spray kept me going for an hour, then my thigh tightened so much that I had to go off.

Next day in the treatment room my mood wasn't improved by translations of quotes from the unrepentant Smith: 'Ardiles and others like him have joined the toughest League in the world and will have to take the knocks. How they react is their problem, not mine. I was just making my presence felt as I've done before and as people have done to me. The tackle was a bit late but it was straight-forward, making clear to Ardiles that he wasn't just playing against a Third Division side. It was to say "This is a man's League" – and he didn't like it. I don't think he'll last until Christmas.'

I couldn't train for the remainder of the week; there was a lump like a small orange on my thigh and hours of heat treatment were needed to reduce it. I wasn't fit for Saturday's match at Liverpool but felt obliged to play, as I always do.

I've often played with injuries when it would have been wiser to stay on the physiotherapist's table. Sometimes the pain vanishes and the risk is justified but more usually the outcome is a bad game. From experience, I know it's best not to play when doubtful about one's fitness but, at the same time, a professional can't help choking on the words: 'Leave me out.'

So I played at Anfield. Afterwards, I felt that I never wanted to play anywhere again. We'd been awful, all of us. Liverpool, though, had played like men from another planet. Kenny Dalglish and David Johnson each scored two goals, Terry McDermott and Ray Kennedy each scored one. A penalty by Phil Neal made it seven.

We travelled home in almost complete silence. I was deeply depressed and imagined us being relegated; if that happened, my own inconsistency would be partly to blame.

My introduction to English football was proving harder than expected and the blame for that couldn't be heaped on my team-

*Tommy Smith, the iron man of Liverpool and later of Swansea. He injured me with a late tackle and then forecast: 'This is a man's League and I don't think Ardiles will last in it'*

mates. Tottenham had some really good footballers in Glenn Hoddle, Steve Perryman and Chris Jones. 'We shouldn't be in any danger of going down with players like that, as well as myself and Ricky,' I decided. 'Nor will we win anything yet, but we ought to finish about mid-table.'

I couldn't blame language difficulties for my form. We understood each other on the pitch. When I called 'Here', I was given the ball – even, as my team-mates became used to me, when closely marked. At first, they wouldn't pass when a defender was tight and I could see them thinking, 'He'll only lose it', but I soon convinced them of my ability to beat the man and keep possession.

I couldn't blame the English programme. Two matches a week is plenty, especially if you're carrying an injury, but South American teams play just as many, if not more. Flamengo of Brazil, for example, were playing their seventy-seventh match of the season when beating Liverpool 3–0 in the 1981 World Club Championship. No English club will play that many, even when heavily involved in Europe and Cup replays. Sixty-five competitive games in a season is about the absolute maximum for a Football League side and very few teams have ever played more than sixty, but I wouldn't try to deny that there's an important difference in the physical demands. Latin football is played slowly. The English game is played flat out and is far more taxing.

There was no escaping the truth on the road home from Anfield. The problem at Tottenham was myself and Ricky. We weren't doing the job that English football required from midfielders. We had persisted in playing the Argentinian way, marking space and leaving the defending to the back four. We saw our job as staying up front to keep the attacks moving; when our immediate opponents went on a run, we followed only part of the way. Only in dire emergencies would an Argentinian midfielder get behind his specialist defenders.

The laws of football are the same the world over and so are the players, but styles vary from country to country and we hadn't adjusted. The problem was exacerbated because the whole team was trying to settle into the First Division after a season in the Second.

Our most skilful midfield group was Glenn Hoddle, myself and Ricky, but Keith Burkinshaw was reluctant to play us together. 'None of you win the ball,' he said, which was correct at that time. One of us, usually Glenn at the start, had to be left out while we fielded John Pratt for his tackling.

As well as not winning the ball and coming all the way back to defend, Ricky and I were in conflict with English attacking ideas. We liked to run through defences, playing one-twos to keep possession. The English way is to race for the line and fling over a cross into the goalmouth; it's a tactic that calls for something against our instincts – running into space without the ball.

Eventually, as at Ipswich under the influence of Arnold Muhren and Frans Thijssen, an international marriage was arranged between the two schools of thought. Muhren and Thijssen convinced Ipswich they could attack more constructively by playing through midfield in the Dutch way, instead of hitting balls over the top of it. Ricky and I persuaded Tottenham to use a more varied attack, South American short-passing intermingled with long crosses because that suited the new mixture of players better, and systems have to fit the talent available.

We didn't get it right overnight. There were bad days ahead, particularly a 5–0 hammering at home by Arsenal just before Christmas 1978. They were strong that season, going on to win the F.A. Cup; Liam Brady was superb and Alan Sunderland, who lived in the same road as Ricky and me, scored a most unneighbourly hat trick.

Nowadays I wouldn't dare go out if we lost 5–0 to Arsenal, but at that time, being still new to London, I felt more ashamed about only drawing – and rather luckily, too – against the part-timers of Altrincham in the F.A. Cup. The replay was a different story. It was staged at Maine Road, Manchester City's ground, and we were brilliant in a 3–0 win. I had my best game since arriving in England and we were in a Cup run, beating Wrexham and Oldham before losing to Manchester United at Old Trafford in a replay.

My belief that I was starting to get my game together was endorsed by the results of two major ballots; I finished second to Kenny Dalglish in the Footballer of the Year poll by the Football Writers Association. And I finished third behind Tony Currie and the winner, Liam Brady, in the Professional Footballers' Association's voting for their Player of the Year.

Off the field, things had gone satisfactorily. Ricky and I had found two houses not far from Spurs' training ground. The address sounds more suitable for cricketers: The Oval. A quiet spot, miles from the big shops and the bright lights, but with the overriding attraction that identical houses, side by side, were for sale. Ricky and I wanted to stay together; we thought it best for our wives, Sylvia and Cristina, to be close while they settled down to life in England, and we wanted to stay on an equal footing.

I dreamed of Wembley once we reached the sixth round of the Cup, but United's 2–0 win put paid to that. Our season was as good as over with two months still to go. But, all in all, as an introductory English season it wasn't bad. Two wins in our last two League matches hoisted Tottenham to eleventh in the table. Exactly half-way, just as I'd predicted eight months earlier on the way home from Anfield.

# 7 REFEREES

I swore at referees throughout my first season with Tottenham, but they never booked me because I swore in Spanish. What a difference, though, when my English improved! Only five months into the second season I'd collected eighteen disciplinary points for dissent, only one wrong word short of an automatic suspension; I then took a grip on myself and shut up. There were no more offences.

In a way, my record for dissent could be compared with passing a language examination, except that I'm not proud of the language I was using and wouldn't wish it reproduced here. Flaring up at referees is among my worst faults. I know I shouldn't do it and I'm always telling myself to calm down but it keeps on happening, even, sometimes, when I know the referee is right.

I feel so ashamed after being booked, realizing that I've lost my self-control again and failed once more in simple human understanding; in other words, I haven't regarded the referee as someone who can make honest mistakes as easily as the rest of us. Once in a match at either Coventry or Leeds, I can't remember which, my abuse of the referee was shocking. I felt dreadful about it when I came to my senses and I wanted to write to him to apologize. Somehow the letter wasn't sent and I'm still looking for that referee to express my regret personally.

I owe a similar apology to Clive Thomas which dates from the F.A. Cup semi-final against Wolves at Hillsborough, Sheffield, in April 1981. Wolves equalized in the last minute with an undeserved penalty, scored by Willie Carr. I've seen the T.V. replay several times and have no doubt that Mr Thomas made an honest mistake, as he probably realizes himself by now, but his error doesn't excuse my shocking outburst. The old, red mist fogged my brain and I called him every bad name I had heard in England. He was very decent about it and only booked me although I deserved to be sent off.

There is a borderline in these matters that is unmarked yet recognized by everyone in the game – and we know how far different referees will let us go before taking a player's name. In general, South American referees are stricter than the British, as I know to my cost, having been sent off several times in Argentina for disputing decisions – once in the eighty-fifth minute of an international match against Mexico.

I feel particularly guilty about abusing English referees because their standards are so high. Here I can take the field with total faith in the referee's impartiality; I know he won't be one of those homers who act as referees in some countries. Every British player can kick off with a reasonable hope of winning away from home, but there are countries where refereeing bias would make such a hope futile. No League player has to worry 'Is the referee a bandit? Has he been got at?' It's a fear not unknown in one or two Mediterranean countries, but no one playing under an English referee need ever think about it. A good thing, too. Nothing would kill football faster than corrupt officials.

English referees are excellent at dealing with retaliation. You know what happens: two players go for the ball and the one who is beaten may foul his opponent quite hard out of frustration and he is then pushed or punched in return. In Argentina, the second man is often sent off while the first stays on, pretending to be the injured party. English referees show a clearer understanding of the game, and are usually content to separate the contestants and perhaps book both of them – a fair decision because they are equally guilty.

I would never advocate giving footballers a licence to lose their tempers but, at the same time, it has to be recognized that players are bound to boil over from time to time. The English way of handling these clashes is the most sensible that I've encountered because it avoids ruining matches through needless dismissals. I think that the English way also has the right amount of sympathy for offenders. It is not fully understood by outsiders that the player who is continually boiling over in a match and getting himself into

*Referee Clive Thomas could have sent me off, instead of only booking me, when I called him every bad name I had heard in England*

trouble is not a villain but, more likely, a lad who is thoroughly out of form and angry with himself because of it. A player who is in top form very rarely does anything that might merit being sent off.

There is only one branch of the game in which I believe English referees lack expertise, and that is in their control of the early stages of a match. Hardly any referee in Britain is firm enough in the first ten minutes, which are often a free-for-all. English players cherish the notion that no one is ever sent off in the first minute and they trade on it. The game here will improve rapidly when stricter refs show them they're mistaken.

I was glad when refs began to penalize professional fouls more quickly, not just the trips calculated to an inch outside the penalty area but also the shirt-pulling, which is more widespread than fans may realize. There's also a lot of obstruction caused by tugging a man back by the arm or blocking his path with an outstretched arm. Really serious offences should not be given the name 'foul', but should be seen as what they are: criminal assaults. This happens when the tackler has no interest in the ball but only in digging his studs into the other man's shin. Happily, it's less common than it might be because English football, although hard, is generally fair and not rough in comparison with the Spanish and Italian Leagues. You can go into a tackle with most English professionals confident of playing with gentlemen, but there are a few of whom you have to be careful. They don't go for the ball. I don't know how they can look another player in the eye.

I commit fouls, I lose my temper with referees, but I never stop trying to control myself with the thought that it's only a game and should be played in a sporting and gentlemanly manner. If it isn't, the essence of the game is lost. A certain nastiness, in the sense of being physically competitive, is essential in football but I think most of us understand that it has to be kept within a certain limit, and that limit is transgressed by anyone who deliberately kicks or intimidates people.

I'd like to see referees and law-makers combine to wipe out the offside game. Too many teams care less about using the ball constructively than they do about trapping the opposition through a linesman's flag. Every week wonderful goals are disallowed on technicalities because the defence has run forward.

A beautiful goal was scored by Kevin Keegan against Manchester United in December 1981 at Southampton. He shot over his shoulder from twenty yards but the goal was disallowed because David Armstrong was judged offside near the penalty spot. Armstrong wasn't interfering with play in my opinion because the ball was heading for the 'keeper from a much wider angle. I wouldn't have disallowed Keegan's goal; in fact, I wouldn't give anything to an offside trap because that just isn't football.

Football would have more rhythm and less frustration if the offside game were outlawed; instead, the authorities seem more concerned about the trivial issue of goal-scorers being kissed by their team-mates. It makes me wonder if the men at the top have any true feeling for the game.

When a winning goal is scored, emotions are unleashed and players must be allowed more than a polite 'Thank you'. Football is communal celebration with the goal as its pinnacle, and there is nothing more natural than for players to kiss and hug and share their joy with the fans by running to their end of the ground. Yet there have been cases in Argentina when captains have been booked because their players have run behind the goal to salute the fans after scoring. In one match it happened twice and the unfortunate skipper was sent off. Ridiculous!

I heard first-hand about the clampdown on kissing when I re-joined Argentina for one match in April 1979. It was a replay of the World Cup final against Holland staged in honour of F.I.F.A.'s seventy-fifth anniversary. Their headquarters is in Switzerland, so the venue was Berne which thus became the scene of Diego Maradona's European début.

F.I.F.A. presented all of us with solid, expensive wristwatches as souvenirs. I still wear mine but haven't yet had my name engraved on it; I didn't put my name on the match, either. It was good, close and goal-less, but I'll remember it as one of my worst. I even missed a penalty when we tried to settle it with a series of spot-kicks. I used to take penalties for Argentina but gave up the job after missing a couple. Penalties are a matter of confidence; without it, you'll never score.

We tied at 4–4 in the first round of penalties against the Dutch, so we started on sudden death – and I missed one. I'd run a lot in the match and I was tired. As I went to kick the ball I was attacked

*Following pages: Why I hate matches decided on penalty shoot-outs – here I am stretched out with cramp in Switzerland after a miss against Holland in the F.I.F.A. anniversary match*

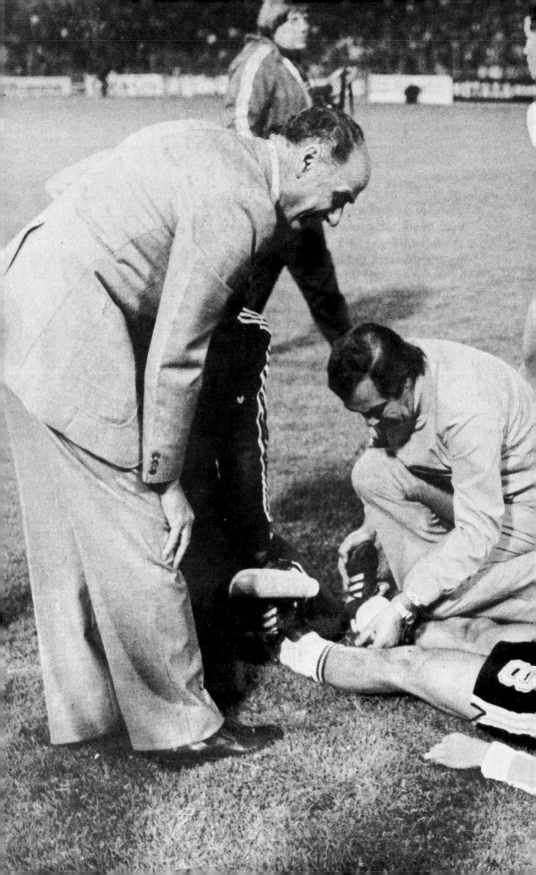

by a spasm of cramp. I should have stopped and gone back to re-start my run; instead, I shot weakly and the 'keeper saved it. I was on the ground by then, crippled by cramp and hoping no one thought I was using that as an excuse for the miss.

Fortunately, Fillol saved the next Dutch penalty, enabling us to win in the end, but even that didn't lift my depression. I was weary and out of form; I'd played too many matches, I hadn't fully recovered from a bout of flu and I was still grieving over the Cup replay defeat by Manchester United a month earlier.

Keith Burkinshaw took me aside, saying: 'Ossie, you're tired. You've lost a bit of concentration and you need a rest, so I'm leaving you out of the match at Arsenal.'

There are only two ways of curing a loss of form: either you play through the bad patch or you take a week off, not even reporting for training. The complete break is probably best for me because every season – along with Steve Perryman and Glenn Hoddle, two others who are rarely injured – I play more than the average number of games for Tottenham.

I wasn't upset about being dropped as I knew it was for my own good and, more importantly, I knew I'd be back; I didn't have to worry about regaining my place. It's the player without that certainty who demands a transfer as soon as he's left out.

A free week meant an opportunity to see more of England; not just for myself, my wife and the boys, but for our regular quota of guests from Argentina. My house is like a small hotel, especially at holiday times. For instance, at New Year 1982 I was putting up a friend as well as my sister-in-law, mother-in-law and grandmother-in-law, and, of course, everyone expects to be shown round.

I usually take my guests to Windsor and Oxford and to my favourite small city, Cambridge. I love it there, it's so beautiful and civilized with that incomparable combination of old buildings and carefree youth; in my opinion, there's nowhere better in England, apart from London itself.

I've done my tourist guide act so often that I probably know London, particularly the West End, better than most London footballers and I've come to appreciate what Doctor Johnson meant when he said that a man who's tired of London is tired of life.

My visitors are always impressed to find me driving quite happily on the wrong side of the road and coping with distances in miles. Oddly, the switch from kilometres never bothered me much, unlike

English weights and measures. I still can't express my weight in stones and pounds and when asked my height, I have to say: 'One metre seventy centimetres.' I don't know what that is in feet and inches.

Supermarkets solved any problems we might have had with shopping. We could see what we were buying even when we didn't know the words for the item or the quantity. I suppose Tesco and Sainsbury are to blame for the fact that my English vocabulary still doesn't include the names of many vegetables. Difficulties in shops in the early days arose only when I wanted something that was not on show or when I tried to replace a breakage without knowing the word for whatever might have been damaged; in such cases I could always turn to the club for help.

The summer of 1979, my first full one in England, gave me time to settle down and survey the astonishingly varied sporting scene – Severiano Ballesteros became the first Spanish golfer to win the Open championship, and Essex, where I'd had my first home, won the county cricket championship. Spurs even got me into whites for their annual match in Hertfordshire; perhaps they thought I'd never heard of the game before but, in fact, cricket is played to a good club standard around Buenos Aires although mainly by Anglo-Argentines.

I enjoyed cricket and learning to play golf but football is my game and I was mad keen to help Tottenham finish higher than halfway up the League table. Instead, the new season brought us down to earth with a bump as we lost the first three matches.

Middlesbrough beat us 3–1 at White Hart Lane on the opening day of the season and, a few days later, we lost 4–0 at Norwich City. At this point, Keith Burkinshaw took me, Glenn Hoddle and Ricky Villa aside, saying: 'We're too loose in midfield and that's why we're letting in so many goals. One of you three will have to drop out.'

In the end, the axe fell on Ricky. He was shocked and refused to be the substitute for the next match at Stoke. He was out of the side for a few weeks. Dropping Ricky made no difference because Stoke City, who had just been promoted from the Second Division, beat us 3–1. Their manager, Alan Durban, jibed: 'Spurs are like British Leyland. They have too many of the same model.'

We ended August 1979 at the bottom of the table without a point after conceding ten goals in three matches. I was depressed although not to the point of prematurely fearing relegation, but I was worried about the team. It's not nice being bottom of the League. The first win seems beyond reach and striving for it takes a lot out of the players. They say winning is a habit, but so is losing – after three successive defeats at what should have been a hopeful time it becomes easy to imagine that you'll never win again.

Our luck changed in the League Cup against Manchester United. They beat us 4–3 on aggregate over the two legs, but at least we won the first one at home. That was enough to change the mood of the club as we followed up that victory by beating Manchester City in a League match. By the beginning of October, we had climbed out of the bottom three, never to return.

The problem at the start was another example of the difficulties that can arise from fitting a new player into a team – in this case, Terry Yorath, captain of Wales.

Yorath had been bought from Coventry City for a reported £275,000 fee as the season was about to start. He was a very experienced player with a biting tackle and the sort of indomitable character that we needed at the time. I expected him to play as the ball-winner in midfield where we'd been too gentlemanly; instead, he played as sweeper for the first three matches but was a bit too slow for the position.

Keith Burkinshaw was shuffling the team around that August, searching for the winning combination. For instance, our right-back at Stoke was Colin Lee who had joined a couple of seasons earlier as a centre-forward; Steve Perryman, who had been the sweeper, was moved to the anchor position in midfield; Ricky Villa was left out; and I was playing as the right-flank striker.

We didn't get it right until Yorath was switched into his best position as the hard man in midfield. He did well for us there, yet I don't think it's necessary for a midfield to be built around a ball-winner. There are better ways of gaining possession than just clattering the opposition with a mighty tackle. Really top-class players can steal the ball and don't need to battle for it. If I had to choose between skill and tackling, I'd sacrifice the tackler.

Tottenham finished the season fourteenth in the table, slightly down but fairly satisfactory after such a dreadful beginning. I was delighted with my own form in the second half of the season and I regard the months between January and May 1980 as the period of my very best football in England.

I was placed in the top six for the Professional Footballers' Association award as Player of the Year, which was won by Terry

84

*I'm just fooling around at golf here but later it became a passion*

McDermott of Liverpool. I was third in the Footballer of the Year ballot by the Football Writers' Association, which was also won by McDermott; I was the overall winner in the *Sunday People* Merit Awards and voted Footballer of the Year by the Tottenham Supporters' Club.

The omens for 1980 as an outstanding year had been correct from the beginning when I scored the winning goal in extra time in an F.A. Cup replay at Old Trafford against Manchester United. It was victory against the odds because we were trying to hold off United with Glenn Hoddle as our emergency 'keeper. Hoddle had gone into goal because Milija Aleksic had been taken off with a broken jaw, some teeth missing and ligament damage after a crash with United's ferocious centre forward, Joe Jordan.

There's nothing like the Cup, though, for catching you out. My good deed at Old Trafford was forgotten two months later when my mistake put us out of the competition in the sixth round. I tried to clear when under pressure at a corner; instead, I mis-kicked and the ball bounced. McDermott, a specialist on the volley, banged it straight into the net. At the end of the month we beat Liverpool in the League, but somehow it wasn't the same.

Hoddle scored twenty-two goals, many of them spectacular, for Tottenham in the 1979–80 season, an impressive total for a midfield player and more than our various front men, such as Chris Jones, Gerry Armstrong and Mark Falco, totalled between them.

I had great faith in Jones. He's superb technically and only a shade behind Hoddle in natural ability. He's also an example of the fact that scorers are born and not made. Strikers are always the first to be blamed when a team is bad – and we were bad two games out of three in that season – but, even so, I think Jones, who is so good in the air, would have done better than nine goals in thirty-seven League appearances if he'd really had the knack. Perhaps he needed the right partner, but I think it's more likely that he felt crushed by the obligation to score goals. Pressure overcame him, as it does so many and, after a long spell out through injury, he was given a free transfer in the summer of 1982.

A team can go only so far without a match-winner. Arsenal are proof of that since the departure of Liam Brady and Frank Stapleton. They've perfected a tactical system that demands a lot of running and makes them difficult to beat. All matches against Arsenal are bound to be tight, but they won't win as many as they ought to until

*Tottenham were too gentlemanly in midfield until they signed Terry Yorath, captain of Wales*

*Steve Archibald is very sharp at sneaking the fifty-fifty ball away from defenders*

they find someone else like Brady who does the unexpected.

Our problem was rather different. We had the individuals (Glenn Hoddle, Ricky Villa and, I suppose, myself) but without the machine-like system and without a guaranteed goal-scorer. It cost a reported £1,400,000 to put that right when Steve Archibald was bought from Aberdeen and Garth Crooks from Stoke City. I already knew Crooks; he'd headed the first goal against us at Stoke in that bad August and scored the penalty with his left. He also set up the third goal for Brendan O'Callaghan.

Archibald cost £800,000 and was London's most expensive footballer at the time of signing, yet only a couple of years earlier he'd been playing as a £7-a-week part-timer for Clyde while running a service station. He's a qualified Rolls-Royce mechanic.

Crooks and Archibald were instant successes. With their help we scored eight goals in our first three matches of the 1980 season. We were top of the table exactly a year after being at the bottom. They have different styles. Steve Archibald has a great appetite for goals. He is very sharp and scores them from nothing, sneaking the fifty-fifty ball away from defenders and always lurking around the box for a chance. Until Steve came, we never seemed to score many 'scruffy' goals – those tap-ins that bounce into the net off a knee or a shoulder. Our goals tended to be elaborate and breathtaking; it was always the opposition that scored the little goals – and beat us as a result.

Garth is the more technical of the two. He creates a lot of chances for Steve, many more than Steve does in return. I'd say that Steve is the more natural finisher of the two as he plays a bit further up front than Garth and makes scoring look easy – which it isn't!

The moment I saw Crooks and Archibald together I knew that Tottenham were in business at last. All we had to do was to stop the opposition because they certainly wouldn't stop us. Goal-scorers usually run out of steam for a spell at some stage of a season, but neither Steve nor Garth did. They scored forty-seven goals between them and the 1981 F.A. Cup was ours.

*Garth Crooks. When I saw him team up with Steve Archibald, I knew that Tottenham were in business at last*

# 8 THE MUNDIALITO

My route into films extended across some 8,000 wearisome miles via
Córdoba, Buenos Aires, Madrid, Zurich and eventually Budapest,
but at the end of it I met a bit-player who up-stages stars. His name is
Pelé. We had parts as prisoner-of-war footballers in *Escape to
Victory*, the imaginative story of a showpiece soccer match staged in
Paris to glorify Nazi footballers at the expense of the multi-racial
prisoners. The big names on the posters were Silvester Stallone and
Michael Caine, but the people of Hungary (where we were filming
on location) disagreed with that: Pelé was their man.

He had hardly kicked a ball for Brazil since the 1970 World Cup
final but his fame was undimmed. The same scene was played every
day at the MTK (Budapest) ground which had been filled with
20,000 extras for the crowd scenes and mocked up to look convincingly French. Michael Caine would arrive to no more than a murmur
(I wondered if anyone in Hungary had heard of him). Stallone,
perhaps because of the two 'Rocky' films, always arrived to a little
handclapping and scattered cheers. But Pelé, scorer of 1,000 goals
and a winner in three World Cups, brought the house down daily.
He loved it; with arms upraised in the centre circle and those huge
eyes beaming, he would turn slowly to all sides of the pitch.

He was still amazingly fit for a man of forty. I studied him closely

Opposite: *Pelé and Bobby Moore exchange shirts in Mexico after
Brazil's 1–0 victory against England in the 1970 World Cup. These
old rivals were still drawing crowds a decade later when I joined them in
Budapest to make the film* Escape to Victory

throughout what turned out to be a week of mainly five-a-sides for the footballers in the cast, but I didn't pick up any tricks. Pelé's style doesn't require them; he was just born with the ability to accept the ball instantly from any angle, and the rest is what I'd call perfect simplicity.

I had been approached about the film after playing in a match at Ipswich. 'O.K.,' I said, although it meant cutting short my 1980 summer holiday in Argentina to join Pelé and Bobby Moore in Budapest. Within the next twelve months, as well as taking part in a film, I was destined to make a record and start writing a book, but I foresaw none of that when I accepted the contract.

They cast me as Carlos Rey, a captured Foreign Legionnaire, complete with a *képi*. It was a speaking part until I protested. 'Look,' I said, 'I'm not an actor and my English isn't good enough.' So I became silent Carlos and looked such a waif in uniform that I couldn't keep a straight face at the preview.

The old England international, Mike Summerbee, was in the cast, as well as internationals from Norway, West Germany and of course Hungary. Ipswich Town sent a strong contingent led by their Scottish international, John Wark. Michael Caine's playing double was Kevin Beattie, the Ipswich and England defender who retired prematurely in 1981 after a series of injuries.

Stallone's double was the Ipswich goalkeeper Paul Cooper, but Cooper didn't appear in the film because Stallone decided to do his own goalkeeping. He had almost no idea about football which was a drawback he shared with the film's directors. They needed continual advice and correction from Pele and Moore. The two of them scoffed at suggestions for spectacular fouls like pushing over the referee and they were always trying to convince the film chiefs that realistic goals only come naturally, they can't be plotted and rehearsed and diagrammed, as the director and his assistant imagined.

I had first-hand experience of this football ignorance one day when a prisoners' training session was being filmed. As Carlos Rey I beat two or three defenders and raced for the by-line but, as the ball began running away from me, I had to stretch and slide for it. My right leg was at its full extent when I made contact again but, somehow, I clipped the ball into the goalmouth where it hit the crossbar and spun into the net. It was the goal of a lifetime. The assistant director agreed.

94

'Tremendous, Ossie,' he cried. 'Exactly what we want, but we didn't get it on film. Would you mind doing it again?'

The film people, though, were expert at their own business of organizing and feeding their vast crowd of extras and at arranging the special effects. They transformed an ordinary Iron Curtain stadium into a wartime French ground. They were fully aware of the risk of anachronisms like Adidas shirts or boots with Puma stripes; all manufacturers' insignia were removed from our equipment and because Paris in the film was supposed to be cold, we had to kit up as if for winter, although Budapest that summer was scorching.

The match sequence lasts only about ten minutes in the film but the shooting took eight days and a lot of the time was spent just messing around while cameras were moved.

Silvester Stallone's goalkeeping was another cause for delay. He needed nearly three dozen attempts to save a penalty from the German captain. I'm afraid his famous team-mates (Pelé, Moore, Wark and myself among them) were also partly responsible for the scene taking so long. The problem was boredom; we'd simply lost interest in Silvester flinging himself around the goalmouth, so when he stopped the ball after a dozen attempts the cameras showed the rest of us lounging around, yawning and chatting instead of leaping and rejoicing! Poor Silvester, he had to do it again. And again.

Six months after saying goodbye to Pelé I was back home in South America sharing a dressing-room with the boy who has earned the title of World No. 1 footballer – Diego Maradona. We were in the Argentina squad preparing for a tournament in Uruguay called the Copa de Oro, or Gold Cup, but more commonly known as the Mundialito, or Little World Cup.

This six-nation tournament was to celebrate the fiftieth anniversary of the inaugural World Cup which had been staged in Montevideo, the Uruguayan capital, in 1930, and been won by the hosts. The invited six were the élite former winners: Uruguay, Brazil, West Germany, Argentina, Italy and England. Objections by the League clubs forced England to withdraw, however. Manager Ron Greenwood would have been unable to raise a full side and so Holland, losing finalists in 1974 and 1978, were substituted.

Keith Burkinshaw generously released me from Tottenham for three weeks, so I was the Football League's only representative in the Mundialito. Christmas at home, my first since leaving Argentina, was an attraction for the family and I was also honoured by being recalled by Menotti. I had been only a spectator at Wembley in May 1980 when Argentina lost 3–1 to England; I wasn't at all hurt by not being selected because I knew that Menotti wished to try out new, home-based players but, at the same time, I had an eye on getting my place back.

I headed for Buenos Aires and made no bones about my disappointment over England's absence, saying: 'They've missed a great opportunity, they ought to have come. The game in England is still suffering from the team's poor results in the European championships in Italy last summer. England won only one match, so Uruguay would have been a chance to put things right by reminding people how good English football really is – as I've found by playing in it.'

With hindsight, I might not be quite so definite. Holland, who lack England's stature, proved a poor replacement. The Italians were no better and even the Germans, after a run of twenty-three unbeaten matches, lost both their games.

Menotti recalled Bertoni from Italy as well as me from England so he could field almost all the old World Cup winners or, at any rate, nine of them. Maradona had come into the midfield and there was a new centre-forward, Ramón Díaz, from River Plate, who'd been Argentina's top scorer in a world youth tournament in Japan the year before. Díaz is unusually quick and very skilful but probably needs to improve his concentration and attitude before being able to justify the widely-held opinion that he's the equal of Maradona.

Argentina's preparation was thorough, as usual. The players had been withdrawn from club games for a month's special training and their teams had to manage without them even in cup finals and championship deciders. Menotti threw me into a half-hour practice match less than twenty-four hours after my long flight from London and, from then on, there was a match almost every day against hand-picked, second-rate opposition.

The tournament was tightly scheduled with seven matches in twelve days. The teams were split into two groups of three: Uruguay, Holland and Italy were Group A, and then Argentina, Brazil and West Germany in what looked decidedly the stronger group. The title, plus a £238,000 purse, was to be decided in a knock-out final between the group winners.

All the matches were played in the Centenario stadium, refurbished and freshly painted, but still basically the same as in 1930. What makes it different from other grounds is a tombstone on the far touchline marking the spot where a club president, seeing his team relegated, rushed on to the pitch and shot himself.

The weather was perfect, sunny and hot; the stadium was filled with 65,000 spectators and massed military bands. Thunder flashes and ticker-tape greeted the teams, Uruguay and Holland. The hosts took the Mundialito very seriously; they had been in training for two months. Holland plainly hadn't; they lost 2–0 which meant they were out of the running although still with a match to play.

Two days later we took the field against the Germans. I hadn't been happy with our form in training but we won 2–1. This was the first international defeat for the German manager, Jupp Derwall.

I felt my second-half display was good, although not eye-catching, but full of running and effort on behalf of the team. We won after being behind, which is always satisfying. Hrubesch (whose power in the air won the European championship for Germany in the summer of 1980) headed in from a corner taken after Fillol had palmed away a shot from Rummenigge, the newly elected European Footballer of the Year.

The Germans had decided to mark Maradona closely with Briegel, a burly midfielder, who kept trying to force Maradona on to his (supposedly) weaker right foot. He even shadowed him when Germany had the ball. Briegel handled Maradona cleanly and fairly, earning an indirect tribute a few days later when Maradona told a press conference in Montevideo: 'I need more experience against man-to-man markers of international class. They're catching me too often. My lack of anticipation against them is a major flaw. I'll have to sharpen my game.'

We beat the Germans by changing to open football in the last half-hour. Our equalizer was debited to Kaltz, the German right-back, after a mix-up with his goalkeeper, but I thought Passarella's header from a corner would have gone in anyway. The winner was a wonderful goal by Díaz.

Victory against the Germans on New Year's Day – what better way could there be to start 1981? But, once again, Brazil brought us up short. Our 1–1 draw, in temperatures of over 80° Fahrenheit, was the usual war, typified by Passarella's early foul on Batista, the Brazilian hard man. It's a pity that matches between us do so little good for football.

Maradona put us ahead in the thirty-first minute when he beat off

97

a challenge from Batista. Some neutral observers thought Batista was fouled while others blamed Oscar, Brazil's centre-half, for being slow to cover. However, there was no argument about the shot – a fast, low, right-footed special.

We made all the early running but tired in the second half when Brazil, through the intelligence of their skipper Socrates and the forward running of Cerezo, created a lot of chances. Fortunately for us they couldn't add to Edevaldo's forty-sixth-minute goal from a half-cleared corner.

There was hardly any fuss afterwards about the roughness of the match; I suppose it was considered almost a sporting affair compared with the previous day's brawl between Uruguay and Italy when three players were sent off.

That game had boiled with arguments even before the kick-off. Uruguay's goalkeeper-captain, Rodrigues, never slow to say his piece, began to protest that the ball was too soft. As a result the match started late with the crowd in a bad temper but, fortunately, not violent as British fans often are. Players on both sides were kicked from behind, pulled down by their arms, violently body-checked, hit across the nose. Then, early in the second half, there was a bizarre armistice when both teams stood in a minute's silence for the memory of Gigi Peronace, Italy's cheery little liaison officer, who had died of a heart attack on the eve of the team's departure from Rome.

The truce lasted only long enough for Olivera, Uruguay's centre-back, to get booked for fouling the Italian left-back, Cabrini, and the game turned thoroughly nasty after a sixty-eighth minute penalty by Morales, Uruguay's 36-year-old left-winger. Cabrini fought on the touchline with Uruguay's right-back, Moreira, and they were both sent off. There was more trouble after Victorino, Uruguay's centre-forward, scored a decisive second goal; this time, Tardelli was sent off. It meant he was out of the tournament, but his foul, a waist-high kick that crumpled Uruguay's right-winger, Ramos, deserved something as drastic as an immediate sending home.

Four bookings and three sendings off are the story of the match but, in my opinion, Italy were lucky to have only Tardelli and Cabrini dismissed. I'd have sent two more to join them.

Uruguay's victory guaranteed them a place in the final against either Argentina, unbeaten and with three points, or against Brazil if they could beat West Germany 2–0.

The Germans intended to take the match seriously. They spent a

*Diego Maradona of Argentina is the world's greatest footballer but too much responsibility was placed on his shoulders in the 1981 tournament in Uruguay for World Cup winners*

full half-hour warming up on the pitch and the conditions, cloudy with the temperature down to the low sixties, ought to have suited them, but they were a little disorganized, having lost Hrubesch with glandular fever only that morning, and then Kaltz, with a strain, after only half an hour's play. Despite these handicaps the Germans went ahead in the fifty-sixth minute with a near-post goal by Allofs after a long run along the right by Rummenigge. It seemed that Argentina were destined for the final. Unhappily for us, the lead was short-lived. A dipping, spinning free kick over the wall by Junior, the outstanding left-back, put Brazil level on the hour. Then they attacked the Germans increasingly with crosses for goals by Cerezo, Serginho and Ze Sergio.

Menotti was furious about the German collapse; in less than half an hour they went from 1–0 leaders to 4–1 losers. He knew some of the German players had been sneaking out to nightclubs and commented later: 'They can't have an easy conscience about this result.'

In retrospect, I'm sure he understands that the Germans were in the difficult position of having nothing to play for – if they won, they were playing for Argentina. But if West Germany had been playing for themselves, then not even Brazil could have hoped to beat them 4–1. I think that Jupp Derwall was right when he spoke afterwards of 'a certain lack of motivation in my team through knowing we couldn't reach the final'.

An estimated 600 million people saw the final between Uruguay and Brazil which was televised live to twenty-two countries and, as the average gate for the seven matches was 60,500, the tournament was a commercial success. It was also a triumph for Uruguayan nationalism and a million or more people took to the streets of Montevideo after their 2–1 victory. The goals had been scored by Barrios and Victorino against a penalty by Socrates for Brazil who had pursued the wrong policy of retaliation in the final instead of relying on their superior skill.

To anyone accustomed to British football crowds, it might seem strange that there was only singing and dancing in the city and no violence. All the acrimony seemed to be reserved for the press conferences. I'm not thinking only of the Brazilian radio reporter who was knocked unconscious after being chased by an insulted player. I'm thinking of Menotti blasting the Europeans by saying: 'They were bad professionals in this competition, a disgrace.' That may sound harsh, but the whole Argentinian camp felt that Holland, Italy and West Germany hadn't taken the Gold Cup seriously.

Rummenigge kicked back on behalf of the Germans by declaring: 'Now that I've played against Maradona, I would describe him only as a very good player and certainly not the world's No. 1.'

Maradona was also on our minds when we talked with Menotti about failing to reach the final; I voiced the general opinion when I said 'We left too much to Diego. We thought that in order to win all we had to do was give him the ball. No one, including me, stretched himself.'

While we held an inquest, Uruguay were hailing themselves as 'Champions of Champions', but they were cut down to size eight months later when they lost 2–1 at home to Peru in a World Cup qualifying match. This defeat was instrumental in putting them out of the running for Spain '82.

So the Copa de Oro had a sour sequel for the hosts, as it also had for me. It was entirely my own fault for taking an unjustified liberty. The final was played on a Saturday and I was booked to land back in London on the following Monday; instead, I stayed for a few extra days with my family in Córdoba. Guilt, combined with disappointment over my performance in Montevideo, ruined what had seemed a good idea at the time; I felt uneasy throughout this unscheduled holiday. I didn't bother with any lame excuses when I arrived back in England three days late; I apologized to Keith Burkinshaw, I'd abused his trust and goodwill and I felt dreadful about it.

We were playing Arsenal the following Saturday. He dropped me and was right to do so; the team would have resented my inclusion. No one in the dressing-room said anything to my face but I could sense tension in the atmosphere. Suddenly, after playing in England without any problems, I had put a question mark against my reputation as a good professional. The folly of this self-inflicted damage affected my confidence. I found difficulty in regaining a team place from my stand-in, Garry Brooke, who had played so well in my absence; in fact, I was taken off for him in my first League game back, which was against Brighton. It was almost two months before I began to feel at ease again, and by then we were striding along the road to Wembley.

# 9 WEMBLEY 1981

In our ranks there's Ossie Ardiles
He's had a dream for a year or two
That one day he's going to play at Wembley
Now his dream is coming true
Ossie's going to Wembley
His knees have gone all trembly
Come on, you Spurs
Come on, you Spurs.

That's an excerpt from the lyrics of Tottenham's 1981 Cup song which was called 'Ossie's Dream'. It had a catchy conga rhythm and made the pop charts, selling some 50,000 records and earning us a team appearance on *Top of the Pops*.

It was my first experience of Wembley fever as there is no F.A. Cup in Argentina or any knock-out competiton that attracts comparable attention. Our eventual victory against Manchester City in the replayed final was the springboard for the club's success in the following 1981–2 season when we went back to Wembley twice – in the League Cup final against the holders, Liverpool, and as the holders ourselves in the F.A. Cup final against Queen's Park Rangers. In addition, we had remained serious contenders for the League championship, as well as reaching the semi-final of the European Cupwinners' Cup.

Success breeds success in football as in anything else; the difficult feat is to win something for the first time, a fact not properly appreciated by the many people who believed that we enjoyed an easy path to Wembley in 1981.

There is no denying that the draw did not pit us against any giants of the game. We faced, in order, Second Division Q.P.R., Third Division Hull City, First Division strugglers, Coventry City, and Third Division Exeter City. Even the semi-final gave us the least difficult of three possible opponents in Wolves, who had spent the season battling against relegation from the First Division. Yet playing for a team that hasn't won a trophy for nearly ten seasons and won only two of their nine games immediately before the start of the F.A. Cup makes winning harder than it looks. That statement is likely to be shouted down by objectors (such as Arsenal fans) who'll readily point out that we reached Wembley having played only one match outside London.

That was the first semi-final against Wolves at Sheffield Wednesday's ground. It resulted in a draw because Wolves were awarded a penalty when Kenny Hibbitt fell at Glenn Hoddle's feet in injury time. I was furious with referee Clive Thomas who had lived up to his old nickname of 'Clive the Book' by taking eight names for various offences. Yet unwittingly Mr Thomas had done us a favour because the replay at Highbury gave us a chance to perfect our game, which we did by winning 3–0 in brilliant style.

Andy Gray, the £1,000,000 Wolves centre-forward, had damaged a hamstring in the first match and was ruled out of the replay. 'We've not much to worry about now,' I said on learning the news.

Keith Burkinshaw expressed the same thought, saying: 'It's our biggest stroke of luck.'

You would be right in thinking that there's not much room for sentiment in professional football. This is particularly true at the time of a semi-final which is the worst round of all to lose. No one ever remembers beaten semi-finalists; no one, that is, except the losers themselves, and then only with bitter regrets.

Our first goal at Highbury came with my pass to Glenn Hoddle who lofted the ball for Garth Crooks to head in. The second was a shot by Garth from Glenn's pass, and the third was a twenty-five-yard shot by Ricky Villa.

I was delighted by the general performance; I thought the midfield was outstanding and I was happy at last with my own form. I considered the replay was my best game since returning from the Mundialito in Uruguay three months previously.

We all went out celebrating that night at a hotel near Enfield and never tired of recounting the omens; it was the Chinese Year of the Cockerel, Spurs had never lost a Wembley final, the club always won something in years ending with the number one (the F.A. Cup in 1901, 1921, 1961, the League championship in 1951 and 1961, the League Cup in 1971). But those lucky signs counted for nothing in the final itself when Tommy Hutchison, at thirty-three the oldest man on the field, headed Manchester City into the lead. They held that lead for nearly an hour.

Few sides have recovered from being a goal down at Wembley, so it must have seemed that Manchester City were heading for a fairy-tale finish to a season in which they had seemed certain of relegation. When John Bond moved from Norwich City to become their manager in October, they were bottom of the First Division with only four points from eleven games. The bookmakers were still unconvinced by City's revival and they made us favourites to win the final. Hutchison's goal from a cross by Ray Ransom could cost the public a fortune in lost bets but then Hutchison became the first player for thirty-five years to score for both sides at Wembley; the previous one, I'm told, was Bert Turner of Charlton against Derby County in the first post-war F.A. Cup final.

A lot of people felt sorry for Hutchison and thought his own-goal was bad luck for City. I didn't see it that way; in my view, we fully deserved our replay. Only Joe Corrigan had stopped City from losing first time with saves from Graham Roberts and Tony Galvin around the twenty-fifth minute and a late one from Steve Archibald. Our goalkeeper, Milija Aleksic, had nothing to save apart from that Hutchison header. I agree that City concentrated on their jobs better than we did and they were certainly more aggressive in midfield, but their tactics amounted only to stopping us, the superior side, from playing. Gerry Gow was the keystone of this plan.

Gow was among the first players bought by John Bond when he began saving City from relegation. He is a stocky Glaswegian who cost £175,000 from Bristol City where he had played some 400 games. I imagine the yellow card must have figured in plenty of them. He fouled me almost at the start of the final; when he fouled me again, it cost his team the Cup.

It happened like this: Gow had the ball, I sneaked up from behind and stole it, he then tracked me down but committed a foul in doing so in that dangerous region just on the right of the penalty area. The free kick had been rehearsed to perfection. I tapped the ball, Steve Perryman stopped it and Glenn Hoddle curled a kick at the goal, but Corrigan was ready for him and dived to the left. I've no doubt that Corrigan would have saved but for Hutchison intervening by attempting to block the ball with his shoulder only to deflect it into the other corner of the net.

Extra time proved to be an endurance test. It was half an hour of players collapsing from cramp and the majority of them wore white Tottenham shirts. Wembley's pitch was slippery and heavy that day; also, because of the running track, it seems vast compared with playing areas in the League but I think the explanation of the cramp lies elsewhere. I think it's caused by nervous exhaustion which would explain why players are afflicted so often in the excitement of Cup finals but hardly ever in international matches at Wembley.

Friends were saying to me: 'You've played in a World Cup final, so you shouldn't be nervous,' but I was as jumpy as anyone about appearing at Wembley for the first time. I've played in bigger and more modern stadia – the dressing-rooms, for example, don't compare with those at River Plate – but I've never played anywhere with greater atmosphere and tradition. In Argentina we would call Wembley 'a cathedral of football'.

Superstition had little part in the pre-match proceedings. Tottenham are not a superstitious team apart from Steve Archibald needing to plant the ball in the net before every kick-off and Graham Roberts insisting on being last out of the dressing-room; I'm usually one of the last but that's from laziness, not fear of the supernatural! However, as a devout Roman Catholic, I cross myself on entering any pitch; I did this once at Ibrox Park which has undoubtedly ruined any chance of Glasgow Rangers ever wanting to sign me. It could have been worse, though, for I was about to stroll out for a pitch inspection while wearing a sweater of Celtic green when the other Spurs players shouted 'Get it off! The crowd will go mad.'

There were a full four days to recover for the replay, the first at Wembley itself in the history of the F.A. Cup and the first in the final of the competition since Chelsea beat Leeds United at neutral Old Trafford in 1970. We were glad of the time because we had suffered some damage; Chris Hughton was concussed, Graham Roberts had lost two teeth and Ricky Villa had a broken heart. Poor Ricky had been taken off at Wembley and replaced by Garry

*Ricky and his wife, María Cristina. At three in the morning he phoned me:
Quick, drive us to the hospital the baby's coming'*

Brooke; as a result, he was deeply depressed, as anyone who saw his lonely walk to the dressing-room tunnel would have guessed. It was much more serious than the momentary resentment of being substituted.

To Ricky, that seemed the lowest point in the blackest year of his career: 1981 had gone wrong from the very start for him with an injury while I was away in Uruguay. He thought he'd be out for a couple of matches, but instead it was two and a half months, and he still wasn't right when the plaster came off his leg. This was hardly a good moment for the club to offer him an unacceptable new contract.

'I'm not signing this,' he confided. 'Everything bad happens to me in England, so I'm going home and getting out of the game.' He wasn't exaggerating, I knew him too well to imagine that. We're very close, being fellow countrymen, next-door neighbours, team-mates and true friends.

He phoned me at three in the morning on the day his plaster was due for removal. 'Hurry,' he said. 'Drive me and María Cristina to the hospital, the baby's coming.'

I took them and stayed until six. Mother and daughter María Eugenia were doing fine. Next morning at five, Ricky rang again. 'Hurry,' he urged. 'Stitches have burst, there are complications.' His plaster was off but he still couldn't drive, so once more I took him to the hospital. Happily María Cristina and the baby were all right.

Whatever success we've had in England has been a joint effort. It's easier for two than for one. We go our own ways inside the club, mixing with different sets of team-mates, but off the field our families share birthdays and Christmases and New Years. We know all each other's relatives and we have never fallen out.

Yet sad though it would have been to part from Ricky, I had to face the idea of carrying on alone at Tottenham, especially when he rejected the club's revised offer. April had arrived, his fourth month out of the League side. Then he was picked unexpectedly as substitute against Everton. We were two goals down at half time but Ricky came on to help transform the game after the interval and we drew 2–2 with goals by Garth Crooks and Steve Archibald.

Our next match was the semi-final. He wasn't properly fit, but his knee was improving steadily and he scored against Wolves in the replay. Thoughts of retirement were fast changing into: 'I'd be happy just to be the No. 12 at Wembley.'

Keith Burkinshaw had more ambitious plans for him and put him in the team for a warm-up run against Southampton, Liverpool and West Bromwich before picking him for the Cup final. The story might have ended there in despair and anti-climax but for Hutchison's own goal. The resulting replay rescued Ricky's career.

I was uneasy about the replay. The F.A. had ruled that it would be settled on penalties if the scores were level after extra time; I didn't want that, remembering my miss in Switzerland. Penalty shoot-outs are unfair on the players. Think of Graham Rix against Valencia in the 1980 European Cupwinners' final – his fine display for Arsenal is forgotten, only the penalty miss is remembered.

So I was worried, Ricky was depressed and the fans seemed quiet. This second final lacked atmosphere until Ricky's winning goal. Our supporters went crazy and the press box hailed it as the most brilliant goal at Wembley since one by Ferenc Puskas of Hungary against England in 1953.

Now that I've seen the video and watched Ricky twisting and turning between three defenders I realize that my friend achieved a masterpiece, but at the time it was just a goal to me. The wonderful details didn't register while I was out on the pitch. That goal won national fame for Ricky and no one who saw it will ever forget him. Yet we both know that his first goal was more important. It was just a simple bounce and shot, but it came in the fourth minute of the replay and banished all his fears about giving another bad performance.

Ricky is a confidence player; we all are to some extent. From the moment that first goal went in, his confidence blossomed and he clearly had no doubts about his ability to sell dummies. The real Ricky Villa wasn't often seen before that replay; now he's always on the pitch, as in that 3–2 win against City. Tottenham offered him an acceptable contract almost immediately. It was the workaday first goal that changed his life – not the dazzling second. For without the first, there wouldn't have been the second – and then who knows where Ricky might be now?

We went straight from Wembley to White Hart Lane for a party in the banqueting room under the stand. Bill, our coach driver, came in a borrowed tracksuit. His suit was soaked; we'd thrown him into the bath and George, the second physiotherapist, too. And anyone else we could lay hands on.

Outside, a line of mounted police sealed off the streets as our

*Here is the climax of a goal that has been ranked as one of the best ever scored at Wembley – Ricky Villa, who has already dribbled past two men, shoots as a Manchester City defender and goalkeeper Joe Corrigan try to block the ball. And that was the winner of the 1981 F.A. Cup Final replay*

*We've won the Cup! Glenn Hoddle is holding it with Garth Crooks directly beneath. It's replay happiness for Tottenham at Wembley; then we went off to a club party, but not before throwing our coach driver in the bath!*

fans sounded horns, climbed on car roofs, waved flags from over-crowded lorries and turned North London into a good imitation of Buenos Aires on World Cup night. The F.A. Cup was in a place of honour on the stage except that Garth Crooks was using the lid for a hat, and we all joined in a massed version of 'Ossie's Dream'. Ricky wore an enormous sombrero, Keith Burkinshaw danced, Graham Roberts whistled through the gap in his teeth, but of all the smiling faces in the room, Steve Perryman's was the one most entitled to show happiness.

I've never known a better professional than Steve nor played under a sounder club captain. He had signed for Tottenham fifteen years earlier and Bill Nicholson, then the club's manager, gave him two tickets for the Spurs v. Chelsea final. It was the last F.A. Cup final he saw, although he'd played twice in League Cup finals. Somehow, these don't have quite the same status. So he felt that Spurs v. Manchester City was his final and he involved himself unselfishly in everything.

He sacrificed his spare time to supervising the players' pool; not for himself (he has a good business and doesn't need the money), but because he wanted it run well for the others. When Ricky is out of the team, I share a room with Steve so I've had the chance to study him and his total loyalty to Tottenham. Wherever he is chosen he'll play without fuss – midfield, sweeper, and in the last couple of seasons as a right-back who ought to have been given a proper chance by England instead of making a single appearance against Iceland in 1982. He's been in the dressing-room longer than anyone; he holds the club record for League appearances and shows every sign of setting a record to last until the end of the century. Yet Steve never takes advantage of his long service and his good example is reflected by the other players with the result that Spurs players rarely attract bad publicity. I'm a practising Catholic and I try to testify to my faith by helping charities and giving something back to the community. The majority of footballers do the same; as a rule, we don't cross the street when the flag-seller catches our eye – but I can't imagine anyone in the game doing more than Steve in the way of visiting hospitals and making personal appearances for charity.

He never talks about these good works, so you have to piece the facts together for yourself. For instance, there's the story of an England Under-23 cap that he donated to a function raising funds

*I've never known a better professional than Steve Perryman. He richly deserved the captain's honour of holding the F.A. Cup aloft from the town hall balcony after our triumphant ride through the crowded streets of Tottenham*

in aid of guide-dogs for the blind. It was auctioned for £225 but the buyer's cheque bounced. Steve then paid £225 from his own pocket for his own cap so that the fund wouldn't suffer.

Steve Perryman richly deserved the honour of holding up the trophy at Wembley and in our open-top bus the following Sunday. An estimated quarter of a million fans turned out for our street parade. Sadly, 136 of them finished in hospital or underwent first-aid treatment for injuries received in small-scale riots along the route. I didn't see any fighting because the people on the pavements were intent first on greeting the team. The fighting started after we'd passed, but we heard about it and Steve appealed for order over the loudspeaker, choosing exactly the right words: 'We hear some people have been injured. Please stay quiet. We love you all.'

It's not my place as a visiting player to say how Britain should be run but having played in a Football League match where a Molotov bomb exploded in the crowd I feel qualified to comment on some contrasts with Argentina.

Football violence back home is confined to the pitch and never spreads to the streets. This contradicts the view widely held in England that players cause crowd trouble. Is there too easy access to alcohol in Britain? Well, you can drink round the clock in Argentina but you never see drunken spectators. Perhaps the important difference is that the law in Argentina would crack down harder on hooligans.

# 10 BRAINS v. BOOTS

The Football League, as well as being sprinkled with university graduates like Steve Coppell and Tony Galvin, is rich in players who have gathered lots of 'A' levels – and yet the legend persists that a footballer's brains are confined to his boots.

It's not true. I doubt if there has ever been a great footballer who was also a dimwit and even an average First Division player is often brighter than most of his contemporaries outside the game. Intelligence is a major factor in sporting success; when it is combined with appetite for the game and intense concentration, you have a champion.

Ray Clemence is a case in point; until he signed for Tottenham in August 1981 I had considered him only a moderately good goalkeeper who owed a lot to Liverpool's defensive system. I soon had to revise that opinion on finding that he has the rare ability to raise team-mates to his own high level of concentration; there's no day dreaming when Ray plays. He organizes the back four and keeps everyone on their toes. After some sixty games for England and approximately 600 League appearances for Scunthorpe, Liverpool and Spurs, I wouldn't be surprised if the competitive edge were dulled. Not a bit of it! He still wants to win everything.

Raymond doesn't make many spectacular saves, but he doesn't need to. His positional sense is so good that it usually seems as if the opponent has aimed at him. Whatever success we had in the 1981–2 season was due largely to the way he instilled confidence and experience into our defence.

There are maybe two dozen goalkeepers in England with the same physical gifts of height and agility and with probably as much natural ability as Clemence, yet they remain only average 'keepers while he is acknowledged as a star. In some cases, this is due to diffidence – lesser goalkeepers don't shout and order players around as he does; for the most part, it is because they are unable to match his burning concentration, for that is the quality which separates the winners from the also-rans.

Football's *crème de la crème*, no matter what their shape, size or colour, have certain attributes in common. As personalities they are never big-headed or flash; indeed, they are frequently self-effacing in the extreme, like Mario Kempes or George Best when he started. However, their essential characteristic is a determination to use their abilities to the utmost, with the result that some players have become world stars on limited technical equipment.

Bobby Moore is just such an example. Not much of a right foot, nothing special in the air, and with only moderate pace, yet he captained the winning side in a World Cup final and set a record of 108 England caps. Few people would deny that Moore, from 1966 to 1970, was the best central defender in the world. What made him so? Sharpness of mind and concentration on his job. He sensed developing danger in the first stirrings of attack and acted immediately to counter it. His refusal to be distracted even went to the length of never congratulating a goal-scorer. Hugging and kissing were left to the others while Bobby returned to his position and awaited the next thrust.

Kevin Keegan is another ordinary player with wonderful achievements. He's in the record books forever as having twice been European Footballer of the Year, putting him alongside such technical geniuses as Johan Cruyff, Alfredo di Stefano and Franz Beckenbauer. An analysis of Keegan's style would probably show: left foot, not very good; right foot, O.K. but nothing more; heading, O.K. but not outstanding; pace, quickish, but he's no greyhound. Why, then, has Keegan become so famous, rich and successful? The answer is that he is determined, hard-working and intelligent. I've seen technically perfect players who will never accomplish a tenth as much as Keegan. I respect him for showing how far a footballer can go with the right attitude and character.

Keegan was on my mind as I flew back to Argentina in April 1982 for World Cup training; I wondered how he would fare as captain of

*There's no day-dreaming for anyone when Ray Clemence plays. He is a goalkeeper with the rare ability to raise team-mates to his own high level of concentration*

England in Spain. After nearly four years among them, English footballers seemed closer to me then than even the players of my native land, so I let my mind range over their prospects and possible stars.

Musings of that nature were bound to start with Glenn Hoddle, the finest technical footballer in England. He would stand out even in South America but, as I headed for the airport, Glenn was not established in England's probable World Cup team. He had suffered from the mysterious difficulties of adapting to international football. Kevin Keegan had had the same trouble; so had I. Time is the usual cure but that was running out fast in April 1982, and I favoured making Glenn an automatic choice to give him the confidence that he might have been lacking. Lack of ability was certainly not the problem, as Glenn has everything a footballer could desire: right foot, left foot, skill, vision; he's even good in the air! He is so truly two-footed that, even after four seasons of playing and training with him, I cannot be sure whether his right foot is better than his left.

Personality problems could not be the reason for Glenn taking so long to blend into England's squad. He's not an awkward guy. He's nice, modest, a hard trainer, a serious professional and a pleasure to play alongside. When he delivers his long, curling passes or strikes those goals from outside the penalty area I'm as thrilled as any spectator. Until the 1981–2 season he was probably suffering from the excessive criticism that is often directed at great players. He didn't sweat enough or get blood on his shirt: sweaty shirts are easily acquired, but not all players wearing them can do what Glenn does.

Under the microscope, the only flaw that I could see in Glenn would be a slight lack of pace, but even then he compensates for it by reading the game so quickly. As Bobby Moore used to say about his own lightning anticipation: 'The first five yards are in your head.'

My microscope might also show an occasional over-use of the long ball. Theorists claim that the long pass went out with the bow and arrow, but when performed by Glenn, with perfect accuracy and deadly penetration, it has a future. However, success with the long ball can sometimes lure him into striving for the impossible ball when something simpler would be much more effective. Glenn's short game is incomparable and a mixture of one-twos with long balls would turn him into an even greater player. He will probably arrive at the right proportion of long and short with experience.

Before the World Cup I wondered about his best international

*Kevin Keegan, shaking hands here with Ray Clemence, is an ordinary player with wonderful achievements. He has shown how far a footballer can go with the right attitude and character*

position. He could play on the right, the centre, or the left of midfield (although not as a left-flank runner in the way that Tony Galvin plays for Tottenham). Right side or left both come the same to Glenn. I also had the revolutionary idea that he could fill a position that hardly exists in English football: the *libero*, the free man playing behind the back four. I knew that he tackled firmly and read the game accurately so he wouldn't have much difficulty with the defensive duties, but I would expect far more from Glenn than his being just an English-type sweeper who supports the centre-half.

The *libero* in non-English football isn't the supplementary central defender but the mainspring of the team and usually its most skilful player; the one who starts attacks from the back, like Ulrich Stielike of West Germany and Luisinho of Brazil. Hoddle could do that job marvellously once he managed the double adaptation required in international football – not only adjusting to unfamiliar teammates, but also to strange opponents.

In League games, you know pretty well how the opposing club will play but there's no telling what may be thrown at you tactically by Russians or Peruvians or, as England discovered when they lost in Oslo, even by Norwegians. I knew this would be a particular problem in the World Cup in Spain where the presence of twenty-four nations meant that the eventual finalists might need to overcome the challenge of teams from four continents. England's players had no experience of dealing with such a broad spectrum of styles. They had not qualified for the finals since 1970 and had only one player who survived from the forty named at that time; this was the goalkeeper, Peter Shilton, who had gone out to Mexico with Sir Alf Ramsey's squad but was left out of the final twenty-two.

In Ron Greenwood's position I would find it hard to choose between Clemence and Shilton. They are both a long way ahead of the other contenders and perhaps the only difference is that Shilton is more spectacular than Clemence.

I used to consider English goalkeepers lacked intelligence but have come to appreciate the difficulties of their job as they try to reach hard, fast crosses while impeded both by opponents and their own defenders. Crosses aren't used in Argentinian football although, as you can see every week in England, they can be a deadly weapon. I wouldn't discard the cross or make any drastic alteration to the English way of playing. There's nothing wrong with their style, they just need to combine all aspects of it and avoid over-emphasis

*Glenn Hoddle has every technical advantage that a footballer could desire – yet, as the 1982 World Cup approached, he was still not an automatic choice for England*

on crosses, one-twos in tight areas, or long balls, but try for a continual mixture of the three.

England, I thought while flying out to rejoin Menotti, need not apologize in any way for the quality of their football or their footballers. Trevor Francis, for instance, would find a place in almost any team in the competition. Admittedly, he often plays a lone hand and can be difficult to fit into a system, but I like him. He's intelligent and very quick, England's best forward.

Phil Thompson was another I expected to see in Spain as the best of England's centre-backs. When Dave Watson, Alvin Martin, Russell Osman and Steve Foster were being touted as World Cup centre-halves, I often thought that people in England worry too much about the need for a big man to head the ball. Almost all English players are good in the air so almost anyone can do the heading job; the urgent requirement was for pace at the back.

I often wondered in the run-up to the World Cup why Thompson was not paired with Bryan Robson. Robson is one of those rare players for whom international football seems to come easier than club matches; he is competitive, aggressive, consistent and, although not particularly skilful, versatile.

I thought about Cyrille Regis and put a question-mark against him. As he warms up in his hooded tracksuit, he looks like heavyweight boxing champion Larry Holmes. He has physical power and strength in the air as well as fair skills and the kind of mobility that loses centre-halves. So I'm always surprised that Regis allows himself to be bossed around when the game isn't going his way. A world-class centre-forward (and there is no question that Regis could become one) never surrenders.

I expected that Ray Wilkins, one of the best technicians in England, might enjoy a good World Cup. He had restored bite to his game. I liked him for it when he was at Chelsea but after being transferred to Manchester United he went through a stage of playing too deep and giving many negative balls.

Steve Coppell, his United club-mate, had been in the headlines shortly before the World Cup as being always the first name written on Ron Greenwood's team sheet. This is due to his industry, intelligence and willingness to sacrifice himself for the team, all qualities that outweigh his technical limitations.

I felt that Kenny Sansom might not do himself justice in the World Cup unless he shook off the suffocating effects of Arsenal's system.

Sansom is best when he can be independent, going forward with verve and spontaneity.

My last view of England had been at Wembley in February 1982 when they beat Northern Ireland 4–0, a flattering scoreline for only an average performance. They had been slow at the back and unimaginative in midfield and attack.

Yet given the right preparation, England could have gone to Spain as well fancied as West Germany, who were the second favourites after Brazil in the betting. That view may surprise English players. If so, it is because they are over-awed by the Bundesliga and keep forgetting that Bayern Munich, Hamburg, Cologne and Borussia Mönchengladbach have all been eliminated by English clubs in recent European Cups.

El Salvador, the minnow of our group, couldn't be taken seriously as a World Cup force, while Hungary, the fourth member of the group, looked even less impressive than they had in 1978 and had been beaten twice by England in the qualifying round. The Hungarian team still seemed too dependent on the inconsistent, unpredictable Torocsik and the injury-prone Nyilasi. I thought the last four would be Argentina, Brazil, West Germany and Spain. Quite a lot of people would have found a place for Russia in that list but I've never been convinced by Soviet football even though they have good players, notably Blokhin and Chivadze; in fact, I had an idea that Scotland could put out the Russians. No one in April 1982 seemed to be making many predictions about Scotland's chances and even the Scots themselves were uncharacteristically quiet, but I thought that the team had a strong spine with Alan Hansen at centre-back, Graeme Souness at centre-midfield and Kenny Dalglish at centre-forward. The manager, Jock Stein, whom I don't know personally, seemed to be highly thought of by people whose opinions I respected.

The team's main problem was finding the right partner for Hansen but I felt that was solved by the belated call-up in March 1982 of Alan Evans, the Aston Villa central defender and a player I have always regarded as one of the best in that position. To sum up, my view of Scotland was that they could have a fairly successful World Cup, especially if Steve Archibald found his best form.

I don't regard the Germans as superior in any way to the British. Their morale is no higher and they're certainly no stronger physically; in fact, it was noticeable how frightened Eintracht Frankfurt were of

Tottenham's physical condition when we knocked them out of the European Cupwinners' Cup.

The Germans have fine footballers in Rummenigge, Breitner and Stielike, but there are equal talents in England; the difference is that the Germans deploy them better at international level. For instance, the Germans left for a South American tour in March 1982 and played against Brazil and Argentina but all England could arrange that month was a testimonial match against the Spanish club Atlético Bilbao.

West Germany won the World Cup and two European championships between 1972 and 1980; in the same period, England failed to qualify for two World Cups and two European championships. When they at last got a place in the 1980 European championships in Italy, they won only one of their three matches. But I still say that England's problem is inadequate preparation, not inferior footballers. If the England squad were pulled out of their club games and given three weeks intense training together, you would soon see a difference in their international record.

The betting swung slightly against Argentina in the months just before the World Cup and we went out from 7–1 against to 9–1. I never understood why. At 9–1 I considered us a very good bet. Our opening group was fairly straightforward. Neither on that flight home nor, indeed, during the weeks of training could I imagine any outcome other than Argentina and Belgium qualifying for the second stage.

The 1970 tournament was Pelé's World Cup; 1974 was the year of Franz Beckenbauer. In 1978, the big name was Mario Kempes. Everyone expected that 1982 would see Diego Maradona installed as the undisputed World No. 1 footballer – to which I always added the reservation: 'Only if we win it again.' The star player, the one everybody remembers, always comes from the winning team. For instance, Johan Cruyff of Holland was outstanding in 1974 until the final when he finished with a loser's medal; the world acclaimed Beckenbauer.

Before the 1982 competition began, there were, in my opinion, only two contenders for the title: Maradona and Zico. They would both be under great pressure, particularly Maradona, who would be required to prove himself in his first World Cup at the age of only twenty-one. Zico was eight years older and had the experience of having played for Brazil in the 1978 tournament although he was troubled most of the time by injury. The Brazilian league is the best in the world, not the hardest (that distinction goes to the English), but the league with the highest quality. And Zico is the major star in that league so it goes almost without saying that he is a great footballer; even so, I didn't consider him better than Maradona. I hoped the World Cup would settle the argument.

# 11 THE LEAGUE CUP 1982

The League Cup was almost ours, but with only three minutes to go Liverpool tore it from our grasp. They equalized and went on to win 3–1 in extra time.

It's not easy to live with the pain of defeat in a Wembley final; it was the first such setback in the history of Tottenham Hotspur. I felt very depressed. I considered us all guilty of being over-respectful towards Liverpool. We had worried about what they might do to us instead of thinking of what we could do to them; we had leaned towards defence after Steve Archibald's early goal instead of putting Liverpool under pressure.

Glenn Hoddle hadn't been 100 per cent fit and he was unable to produce what we needed; Tony Galvin was also reduced in effectiveness by a shin injury after a tackle by Graeme Souness. My own form was good although I tired in extra time. Until then, I was full of confidence and enjoyed the compliment that Liverpool's manager, Bob Paisley, paid me when he made Sammy Lee my shadow because I'd had so much of the ball in the first half-hour.

My new position as anchor man means that I'm bound to have a lot of possession. It's not my best position, I feel slightly restricted in it because I can't go forward without worrying about my defensive responsibilities, but it has proved beneficial to the team, so I'm willing to continue in the job.

Some fans criticized Keith Burkinshaw. They thought it a mistake to take off Mike Hazard and send on Ricky Villa in the sixty-fifth minute. In my opinion, that's a case of being wise after the event for

BANK OF ENGLAND
I PROMISE TO PAY THE BEARER ON DEMAND THE SUM OF
ONE
POUND
£1
ER
LONDON
FOR THE GOVR AND COMPA OF THE BANK OF ENGLAND
CHIEF CASHIER
ONE POUND
CN08 344216

£1

ONE POUND

Sir Isaac Newton
1642 - 1727

*Wembley again for the 1982 League Cup final against Liverpool but Ricky and I never guessed that we were striding out to the first losing final in Tottenham's history*

if we had held on to win (as, indeed, we nearly did) the same people would have praised Keith for a masterly substitution.

A more valid point was our tactical use of Hazard, who was played in the unsuitable role of marker on Souness. We all share the blame, not just the management, for we had agreed at a team talk that nearly every Liverpool thrust begins with Souness and so we had to cut him out. Chelsea had done just this when beating Liverpool a few weeks previously in the F.A. Cup.

The reasoning seemed sound at the time but Mike Hazard was the wrong man for the job; he is at his best when his talents have free rein, so the only result of his attempts to shackle Souness was that he himself was put out of the game in his first Wembley final. I felt sorry for him but there will be many better days in his career and I'm sure that some of them will be with England.

On reflection, our concern over Souness typified the attitude that cost us the League Cup. We should have stuck boldly by our normal game of playing Steve Archibald and Garth Crooks as slightly wide attackers with Mike Hazard pushed up in a supporting position between the central defenders; I push up behind him and everyone goes up with me. But Hazard's use as a marker kept him back and forced me further back, leaving Steve and Garth to battle against four defenders; we then became short of players in midfield with only three men against Liverpool's four.

Liverpool's players stood on the pitch talking in the five-minute interval before extra time, but we lay down. This was seized upon as a sign of inferior fitness. That wasn't so. Liverpool were superbly fit, of course, as they always are, but they were no fitter than we were. The difference in the respective condition of the two teams after ninety minutes was that Tottenham were shattered, mentally and physically, by Ronnie Whelan's eighty-seventh-minute equalizer.

We had been hanging on in a game that had been slipping away from us since before half time. We had had only one chance to increase our lead: a shot by Steve Archibald that had been blocked on the line; yet somehow the Cup was still in our hands. Then, suddenly, it was gone.

No one ran more than Whelan in the extra half hour, the goal lifting him and his team mates like a pep pill. I could hardly run at all due to cramp. It cost us a second goal by Whelan.

A Liverpool player was coming to challenge me for the ball so I tried to play an easy pass to Glenn Hoddle. However, my leg was seized by a spasm that caused me to mis-kick straight to Ian Rush. From him the ball went to Dalglish, then to Whelan and into the net. And Liverpool owed their equalizer to a mis-kick by David Johnson. If Johnson had crossed the ball as he had intended, Ray Clemence would have cut it out; instead, the mis-kick went to Whelan who then scored. Such are the accidents that can decide great matches.

Understandably, the club party that night at the Grosvenor House Hotel was a subdued affair where we sat around picking over all the things we had done wrong. My thoughts were still wrapped up in defeat the following day and I refused to watch I.T.V.'s *Big Match* programme of the final; instead I sat in another room playing chess with Ricky.

My younger son, Federico, is still a toddler; he doesn't understand the dramas that face his father every Saturday. Pablo, my seven-year-old boy, had kissed me as I left for Wembley, saying: 'I pray for you to win, Daddy. Good luck, Daddy.' He was very upset when I returned a loser, but he's a lovely boy and tried to console me with another kiss, telling me: 'Never mind, Daddy. You're still the best.'

That was Sunday. By Monday, I was beginning to feel the first stirrings of optimism again. I began reminding myself that Tottenham were still the most entertaining side in the First Division. We had lost playing straight football and had never stooped, as many clubs would have done in our position, to calculated time-wasting in the closing minutes.

By Tuesday, I was looking forward eagerly to our Cupwinners' Cup match in Frankfurt. Footballers are, on the whole, optimistic people, resilient after defeats; and even if they weren't the system allows them no time to feel sorry for themselves. There's always another match, another chance. This is one of the things I like best about the game. And sure enough, although a training accident put me out of the match, we beat Eintracht Frankfurt on a 3–2 aggregate and were all cheerful again at reaching the last four in Europe.

No one could jeer in the 1981–2 season that we had enjoyed an easy run in any of the cup competitions. Tough draws came thick and fast, starting with Ajax of Amsterdam, three times European champions in the early seventies. We had to face Manchester United, Forest, Arsenal, West Bromwich Albion and the League champions, Aston Villa, in the various cups. Not a walkover among them!

*Kenny Dalglish of Liverpool screens the ball against a challenge at Wembley from our centre-half Paul Miller*

*Sylvia, me and our sons, little Pablo and baby Federico, on the day in 1978 when they arrived in England. When I returned as a loser from the League Cup final in 1982 Pablo kissed me and said: 'Never mind, Daddy. You're still the best'*

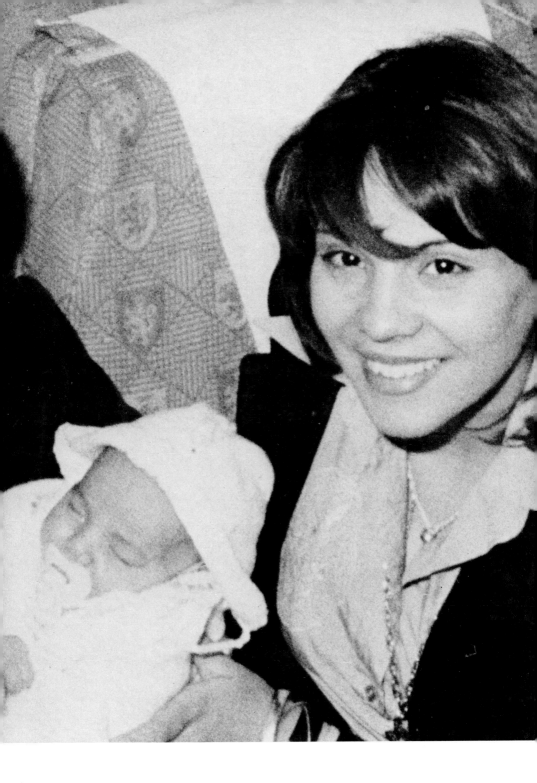

Our victory against Ajax (not the force of old but still able to field some good players) set a pattern that kept repeating itself. We beat them 6–1 on aggregate, playing marvellous football in the two legs and reserving our worst performance for the minnows – Wrexham, for instance. We beat them 2–0 in the League Cup but I'll never know how; I've rarely played in a more forgettable match.

We weren't exactly convincing against Dundalk in the Cupwinners' Cup. Irish part-timers ought not to be a problem for a big English club studded with internationals, yet we won only 2–1 on aggregate.

Fulham, from the Third Division, deserved to take us back to Craven Cottage for a replay in the League Cup. They would have done, too, if I hadn't blocked an equalizer on the line. They lost 1–0 and can consider themselves unlucky.

Our good form returned at Old Trafford against United where a goal by Mike Hazard won the second leg. We beat Nottingham Forest 1–0 in the League Cup. It was 1–0 only because of Forest's goalkeeper, Peter Shilton, whose 'Man of the Match' feats included twice saving penalties by Glenn Hoddle.

A goal-less draw at West Bromwich in the first leg of the League Cup semi-final was another good result, especially as we had to contend with a nervous referee who booked half-a-dozen players for small offences. Naturally, he didn't see the big one – Brendan Batson, the West Bromwich right-back, punching Ricky Villa in the face.

Batson ought to have been sent off immediately; instead, he remained on the field and saw two players dismissed for a later and quite trivial incident. They were Martin Jol of West Bromwich and my team-mate Tony Galvin after a minor tussle on the touchline. Jol, who had been booked once for a foul, held Tony's arm and Tony responded by pushing him across the chest in an attempt to break free. Jol, a Dutch midfielder, admitted shamelessly afterwards: 'I didn't even feel the push but as I'd already been booked and the ref was running up I started holding my chin.'

Two sendings-off and six bookings make the match sound more like a massacre, yet it wasn't at all rough. Nor was the second leg when, with a different referee, we won 1–0 and went to Wembley.

An F.A. Cup win against Arsenal was the best possible way to start the New Year of 1982 even though we owed it to what was probably the worst mistake of Pat Jennings' life. Garth Crooks shot from outside the penalty area, aiming at the corner of the goal. But the ball bobbled along, no force behind it. It ought to have been an easy save but Pat dived over the ball; shortly afterwards he suffered a bad groin injury that was to keep him out of the Arsenal team for three months. It was not a match he will care to remember.

Until coming to England I had never heard of Pat Jennings. Our paths hadn't crossed because he played for Northern Ireland. They hadn't qualified for a World Cup since 1958 which was also the only time they had played against Argentina. But I soon saw why so many football people in Britain, men whose judgment I respect, considered him to have been the best goalkeeper of all time; even at thirty-seven he was still very good and reliable, capable of occasional brilliance and still soaring above everyone to catch the ball one-handed. I always felt that Arsenal had a wall across their goal when Jennings played and, until this Cup victory, we had beaten them only once with him in goal.

Villa were another tough team in the F.A. Cup; we had to give everything to win 1–0. I have a high opinion of Villa: they have solid players and are able to match anyone in both physical effort and skill. I particularly like the midfielder Gordon Cowans, the striker Gary Shaw, and the central defender Alan Evans; I've heard it said that lack of confidence hampers the development of Cowans as an England player. Maybe so, but he would still be in my team.

In the sixth round of the F.A. Cup at Stamford Bridge, Chelsea gave us a shock by taking the lead while we were still at sixes and sevens, unsettled by a late arrival and a wrangle over colours. A traffic jam in the King's Road held us up and we didn't arrive until half an hour before the kick-off. Then, after we had changed, the F.A. ordered us to change our blue shorts for white. We had no white shorts, so we had to borrow a set from Chelsea; we weren't pleased about that as, like all teams, we prefer to play in our own gear.

We were still getting our bearings when Chelsea scored from a free kick. I didn't think there had been an offence but as the referee was George Courtney, a very good official who is on the F.I.F.A. list, I didn't argue, although I had something to say later about his pacing-out of ten yards. 'Can we have the twelve yards that you gave Chelsea?' I asked when it was our turn to take a free kick.

All teams try to steal a yard for their wall; just reducing the distance from the required ten yards to nine provides enormous extra protection for the goalkeeper. Mr Courtney, undoubtedly aware of this, moved us back too far. This caused a heated debate. It's my job, being the quickest off the mark, to dash out of the wall and interrupt the opposition if they try to tap the ball around. Yardage is important to me.

The dispute over the distance was aggravated by the presence of two Chelsea players, Pates and Walker, in the wall. Not unnaturally, Ray Clemence was unhappy with the situation; instead of a rock-steady, defensive line covering his near post, our wall was jostling and wrangling, forcing him to take a position further than normal from his right-hand post. The resulting gap was all that Fillery of Chelsea needed. He shot left-footed down the strong wind and the ball curled in. After forty-four minutes we were one goal down in our defence of the F.A. Cup. It was just what was needed to wake us up.

I had been close-marked in the first half without making much effort to elude my shadow. I changed that after the interval. We pushed Mike Hazard forward, I started making some runs and, within three minutes the scores were level.

A defender handled the ball just outside Chelsea's penalty area, I tapped the free kick to Hazard who teed-up the ball for Hoddle. His shot was too fierce for the teenage goalkeeper. It spun from his hands and the sharpness of Archibald's follow-up did the rest.

A lot of us touched the ball in the build-up to the second goal scored from outside the penalty area by Hoddle. The third goal was another shot from outside the box, this time from Hazard.

Chelsea seized on a moment of slackness in the defence and pulled a goal back in the sixty-fourth minute, but we felt that we had won in style with two beautiful goals in addition to a lot of half-chances. So I was dismayed by the carping criticism of Chelsea's club captain, Mickey Droy, who was quoted afterwards as saying 'I can't understand how Spurs haven't previously conceded a goal in the Cup. They wouldn't have won if Colin Lee and I had been fit to play.'

I thought back to our entrance into Stamford Bridge and the hate in the eyes of Chelsea supporters massing round our team coach. Football isn't about violence and nastiness even though it rouses intense passions. The players and the supporters must always remember the necessity of losing with good grace and of being generous to the winners. I remember the words of Sammy Nelson after we had beaten Brighton 3–1 on their own ground: 'Spurs are

138

the team of the future.'

What had happened to the Spurs players of the recent past? Almost all gone, I realized on looking round the dressing-room that night in March 1982. Only Steve Perryman and Glenn Hoddle survived from the side that Ricky and I joined less than four years previously.

Team-building is a process of continual change as players come and go. It's the same at every club with all the managers trying to piece together their personal jigsaw. For instance, Liverpool didn't sit back after winning the League Cup and the European Cup in 1981. Neither did we after winning the 1981 F.A. Cup. When we met at Wembley in the 1982 League Cup final, there was a total of six new players between us. It shows the turnover that can take place in less than twelve months. They had Bruce Grobbelaar in goal, Mark Lawrenson at centre-back and Ronnie Whelan in midfield; we had Ray Clemence in goal, Paul Price at centre-back and Mike Hazard in midfield. The total expenditure was in the region of £1,600,000, despite two of the six, Whelan and Hazard, costing nothing as products of the respective youth schemes.

Keith Burkinshaw spent £250,000 in the summer of 1981 to sign Paul Price from Luton Town. I wondered at first about the wisdom of the deal because Price is such a withdrawn character, with no obvious passion for the game. However, he has been a star in our back four, even to the extent of keeping out Graham Roberts whom I considered to be the best central defender in England.

I was wrong about Price; I also judged his partner, Paul Miller, too hastily. I first saw Paul after his return from a loan transfer to a Scandinavian club. 'Can't play, not at all,' I thought, but Paul improved amazingly, particularly with his passing. To my surprise he was downgraded to substitute for the F.A. Cup semi-final against Leicester City in April 1982 as Graham Roberts forced a way back into the side.

# 12 CRISIS

My mind wasn't on the game at Villa Park and I remember the final whistle as a signal for relief, more than for rejoicing. We were back at Wembley, we had beaten Leicester City 2–0, but my main thought about the semi-final was: 'Thank God that's over!' It had been difficult to concentrate on playing with my head in a turmoil over the things that were happening eight thousand miles away in the South Atlantic, where Argentinian naval and military forces had just seized the Falkland Islands from the British. Talk about conflicting loyalties – I felt torn in two!

I felt like a prisoner as the media swarmed round our hotel near Birmingham but Keith Burkinshaw and the players shielded me from direct questions and no phone calls were put through. On that day, with Parliament in emergency debate and no decision taken about sending a Task Force, I was hoping for a peaceful solution and saw no need to withdraw from a match that offered us the chance of being ranked alongside the two great Tottenham teams of modern times, the push-and-run Spurs who won the 1951 League championship under the management of Arthur Rowe, and the 1961 double-winning side managed by Bill Nicholson. Nicholson's team were the first this century to win both the championship and the F.A. Cup in the same season; they then successfully defended the Cup by beating Burnley in the 1962 final. We were poised to equal that feat of retaining the Cup, so I couldn't stand down but had to go out and brave a crowd that might be violently anti-Argentinian, for there were reports – false, fortunately – of my house in Hertford-

*Action from my final match in England before the Falklands crisis and the 1982 World Cup. I'm being marked by the Leicester City centre-half Larry May in the F.A. Cup semi-final at Villa Park where a 2–0 victory ensured Tottenham of a record five appearances at Wembley inside twelve months. The games comprised an F.A. Cup final and replay, a Charity Shield match, a League Cup final and another F.A. Cup final*

shire being stoned, and talk that my assets in England would be frozen. I felt as if a bomb had dropped on my well-ordered life.

Warm-ups are not my style – I usually prefer to go straight out and start – so I didn't appear until shortly before the kick-off. I found that the crowd's hostility was swayed by club allegiances rather than national feelings. In other words, Spurs supporters cheered me while Leicester fans booed. I heard the Leicester end chanting 'Argentina bastard!' but was uplifted when the Spurs followers drowned them with: 'There's only one Ardiles!' A short corner between Glenn Hoddle and myself proved the most effective silencer. I flipped the ball into Leicester's penalty area where Garth Crooks volleyed it past the left hand of Mark Wallington, their goalkeeper-captain. That goal ensured our return to Wembley as Cup-holders.

Keith Burkinshaw condemned Leicester's supporters afterwards, saying, 'I'm disgusted by them. We're concerned only with football, not with politics.' It was an attitude maintained that evening when the team gave me a farewell party at a secluded hotel in the Hertfordshire village of Newgate Street. No one argued the rights and wrongs of the invasion, they all simply wished me luck in the World Cup, and Keith assured me: Whatever happens, we want you back.'

Next day, escorted to Gatwick Airport by police and bodyguards, I took off for Buenos Aires. I realized as soon as I arrived there that there was no chance of returning to England to play in the F.A. Cup final even if Menotti remained as willing to release me as he had been before the Falklands crisis. Goodwill gestures were out. Things had gone too far in Argentina.

I've always believed that politics ought to be kept out of sport and I'm sure that almost all sportsmen feel the same way. Unfortunately, politicians see things differently, as any sportsman who reaches the top soon discovers. Politics will then come into his life, riding on his fame, whether he likes it or not. A striking example of this is the United States' boycott of the 1980 Olympics in Moscow. In my case, I was continually thrust into the limelight as an Argentinian international from an English club. 'Ossie, don't go back. Don't go back,' the crowds chanted when I reappeared in the national team. They called for me even before shouting for Maradona. It was a disturbing honour, and such is the emotional power of a direct appeal from 60,000 voices that a return to England seemed unthinkable as I listened to them.

In quieter moments – and there weren't many in those hectic days of the Falklands war – I felt trapped in a family quarrel; Argentinian and proud of it, eager to do anything to help my country, while at the same time loving England as my adopted home. There had never been Argentinians in the English League before Ricky Villa and myself; I liked to think that our careers had brought the countries together for the first time, so I was dismayed by the sudden breach and hoped it could be healed to everyone's satisfaction.

My dual position made me a natural target for journalists; I accepted this role and ducked no questions. Many of the interviews were concerned purely with interpreting attitudes; I would explain to South American reporters how I believed the English might react to certain events and I explained Argentinian viewpoints to English and American writers. The impression has been created that I was anti-British. That's a lie. I never once said anything critical of the ordinary English people. Any reporter who claims otherwise is guilty of misquoting me. My position on possession of the Falklands, though, was pro-Argentinian and I make no apology for that; indeed, I'm proud of supporting my country's claim to the Islas Malvinas, as everyone in Argentina calls the islands. We have disputed British sovereignty for 150 years and regard the islands as part of our homeland. I believe that the Falklands should be returned to us but regret that enough wasn't done to find a peaceful solution. If only the diplomats had talked and talked and talked again until agreement was reached, instead of which war resulted from a series of miscalculations. The English never imagined that we would dare to take the islands by force and we believed that Britain would not bother to fight for them. Like millions in Argentina, I thought the commissioning of a Task Force was a gesture in support of diplomatic moves; even when it sailed, I didn't foresee the shooting. I only began to worry about the outcome when the ships kept on sailing and sailing, closing that gap of 8,000 miles, while each peaceful option, such as the proposals by the United Nations and the personal intervention of Alexander Haig of the United States, was discarded.

All wars are stupid, an insult to man's intelligence. They rarely achieve their objects and usually make matters worse. The Falklands War was particularly stupid in being between countries with similar life-styles who had everything to gain from friendship but had stumbled into hostilities because their governments had adopted positions from which there was no retreat. It was all very sad and I speak as someone who lost a cousin, Flight Lieutenant José Ardiles, in the fighting and as someone who was continually thrust into the limelight as an unofficial spokesman throughout the conflict. The government made no attempt to put words into my mouth. It wasn't necessary because my views, I suppose, were representative of the mood of national jubilation over the seizure of the Falklands. For example, demonstrators who had been calling for the overthrow of General Galtieri's junta changed their tune after the invasion and massed again to acclaim the junta in the Plaza de Mayo, the historic heart of Buenos Aires. It was not personal support for the generals and admirals but support for the cause. I think an eventual solution would be easier if the British people began to understand the almost mystical importance of the Falklands in Argentinian minds.

I believe that the mood in England during the war was intensely pro-British without being anti-Argentinian, which accounts for Ricky Villa being cheered at Wembley as he walked to Spurs' bench during the replayed Cup Final against Queen's Park Rangers. I found a darker humour in Argentina, even in the training camp. 'English' they called me. 'We're beating you now, English,' they would say whenever there was a success for our forces.

I lost touch with England in the seven weeks between the semi-final and the replay. It was difficult to put calls through – I was told there was no communication with London. Just the same, I sent good-luck telegrams to Tottenham before both the final and the replay, as well as before the Cupwinners' Cup semi-final against Barcelona. They never arrived. Yet, despite the war, the lines were not cut and it was a phone call from London to my home in Cordoba that gave me the news of Tottenham's 1–0 victory in the replay. I was glad for the club and grateful for the good tidings although the caller, who had caught me packing to fly off with the World Cup squad to Spain, forgot to mention that Steve Perryman was the new Footballer of the Year and a most deserving winner of the annual ballot by the Football Writers' Association.

I was under a verbal contract to write a World Cup column for a London newspaper. In the circumstances, I decided to forgo it. They understood and agreed to release me. How could I write for an English newspaper when already bound by a public promise not to play in England? I gave that undertaking on Argentinian T.V.

and the consequences were far-reaching for myself and my family.

Let me explain the reasons for ruling out a return to London. It wasn't because of any fears for our safety in England; I felt fairly confident that the English would keep the war and football separate in their minds. (I was proved right a few months later when Ricky Villa began captaining Tottenham in the absence through injury of Steve Perryman. No one, as far as I know, objected and most people thought Ricky was an excellent choice.) War-fever in Argentina, though, was at its height when I went on T.V. there after weeks of quizzing about my intentions. The hostilities were still in the early stages and all the indications were for a long struggle so I announced – understandably, I think – that I would not play in a country at war with Argentina.

Indeed, the armies were still fighting when Keith Burkinshaw came to our World Cup hotel near Alicante. 'I ask you as a friend,' I said, 'please transfer me.'

Keith refused, he said it would break his heart to do so. I replied: 'Mine is broken now, but selling me would be best for both of us.'

He said nothing for a time, then he repeated that he wouldn't transfer me but would retain me on full pay in Argentina. 'Go home when the World Cup is over,' he offered, 'and take all the time you want to think things out. If it's six months or a year, we don't mind. Your contract will be paid until you feel able to return.'

I thanked him for his generosity but objected that his plan wasn't practicable. 'How can I drop out of the game for a year at my age? I'll have to play for someone.'

We talked it over again, anxious to avoid a deadlock. Our positions seemed irreconcilable. Tottenham would not relinquish my registration while, on my part, I couldn't return as though nothing had happened between our countries. We agreed eventually on the compromise of a temporary transfer. 'Just for a year on loan,' Keith stipulated. 'Also, it's got to be in Europe.'

Soccer agents swarmed round when the news got out. Some of them promised me the earth on behalf of famous clubs all over the Continent, but their connections with them were often tenuous and their offers imaginary. However, there were two serious approaches from Italy, two from France and one from Greece. Verona and Sampdoria were the Italian bidders. Verona were the keener. Sampdoria had other irons in the fire, as they showed by signing the former Arsenal midfielder Liam Brady from Juventus of

Turin and, a few months later, the England forward Trevor Francis from Manchester City. Nantes, the leading Breton club, and Paris St Germain were the French contenders. St Germain could offer European competition because they were in the Cupwinners' Cup, as were Tottenham. I was also wanted by Panathinaikos, who were famed as the only Greek club to reach the European Cup final – which they did in 1971 only to lose 2–0 at Wembley to Ajax of Amsterdam.

I knew next to nothing about the five clubs. Verona were offering the best terms, but money didn't come into it as far as I was concerned. The pay is good and roughly the same wherever I play, so I based my decision on other considerations, of which the uppermost was the probable quality of life in the five cities. On that basis, Paris was a winner by a mile and I agreed to join St Germain.

It wasn't long, though, before doubts set in. They came to a head after one of the worst misjudgements of my career, when I allowed myself to be tempted into joining a soccer tour of South Africa. A sum of around £50,000 was mentioned, which is a powerful amount of temptation for a few games. So I was led away, but the sweet talk turned out to be mostly lies. After four years in England, I couldn't plead ignorance of apartheid or of how every attempt at sporting contact with South Africa tended to bring out demonstrators and get questions asked in Parliament. I knew that Test batsmen Geoff Boycott and Graham Gooch had been banned by England for playing in a pirate cricket tour early in 1982 and that their tour had been financed by South African Breweries who were also putting up a million pounds for this soccer tour, which was to take place immediately after the World Cup. I also knew that South Africa were suspended by F.I.F.A., which meant that neither teams nor individuals could play there without themselves risking suspension by their own Football Associations.

I asked about these problems when the organizers sounded me out in Spain. I received reassuring answers but I ought to have known that they wouldn't have been offering so much money if everything had been all right. I asked about F.I.F.A.'s attitude and was told: 'No problems, this tour has their blessing.' I remembered how Boycott's rebel tour had been hammered on the sports pages, so I asked about press criticism.

'No problem. We're calling a press conference in Fleet Street where Jimmy Hill, as the tour consultant, will explain everything.'

I asked about political repercussions.

'No problem. All the matches are being played against multi-racial teams and the tour invitation comes from the black South African F.A.' That bit about the invitation was virtually the only truth they told me.

But I cannot shovel all the blame on the promoters. I'm a big boy and common sense should have warned me from the start that no one offers around £10,000 a match if everything is straight-forward.

I flew to South Africa with Mario Kempes after the briefest of stays with my family in Córdoba; the brevity of that visit home is yet another regret about the tour. My uneasiness grew when we landed at Johannesburg amid such tight security that we were smuggled out of the airport through a side gate and taken to a hotel where more guards kept the reporters at bay. There were moles in the hotel, though, as I discovered almost in the instant of throwing my bag on the bed. A chambermaid looked round the open door and called: 'Son, take care of your career!' Just that, then she was gone.

Dirceu, the thirty-year-old Brazilian who played midfield in the 1974 and 1978 World Cups followed Kempes and myself into Johannesburg. He was a free agent after being released by Atletico Madrid. Two England veterans, forward Mike Channon and centre-half Dave Watson, were also free agents after completing their contracts with Southampton. The only Continental in the party was Fons Bastijns, a Belgian who played right-back for F.C. Bruges in the 1978 European Cup final against Liverpool at Wembley. Bastijns, too, was a free agent and he said: 'As I've also decided to retire after this tour, I'm not worried what happens.' Some of the tourists were free-transfer players like my old Tottenham team-mates, goalkeeper Milija Aleksic and full-back Gordon Smith. The others – although Dirceu, Watson and Channon had been big names – were in the twilight of their careers. Kempes and myself, both fresh from the World Cup, were the only active internationals in the squad. Ours would be the heads to roll. I realized, if F.I.F.A. asserted their authority. Nothing much could be done to the others.

The same thought occurred to Keith Burkinshaw. He rang me in a flaming temper. Keith doesn't swear often but this time he let me have both barrels. In four years, I've never known him so angry. Stripped of four-letter words, his question was, 'What the hell do you think you're doing?' He reminded me that Tottenham still held my registration, and said, 'Catch the first plane out of South Africa.'

The tour team was being run by former Wolves manager John Barnwell and I'm sure that he sympathized with the position in which I had placed myself but, at the same time, he had a job to do, and so I was under a lot of pressure to play in the opening match. Once again, the organizers claimed to have the approval of F.I.F.A. 'But have you got the approval of Tottenham?' I asked. 'I'll play only with their written authorization.' Keith would never give that permission, he had left me under no illusions about that, but he couldn't physically restrain me from turning out if I decided to take the risk. So it was up to me – and the organizers kept pressing right up to the morning of the first game, saying, 'You're a French player now, so an English club can't tell you what to do.'

I replied that Keith wasn't a man who would lie to me or to anyone else for that matter; if he said that Tottenham held my registration, then they unquestionably did hold it.

The tour bosses wouldn't let the matter drop; they were desperate to get me on the field and began urging, 'Play – and we'll fight F.I.F.A. for you if you're suspended. We'll pay all your legal costs and, what's more, we're certain that you'll win.'

I don't like being brusque with people, but in the end I told them bluntly: 'Leave me out. I want to play football without a lot of hassle, not to spend years in courtrooms.'

Kempes, who was being re-transferred to Valencia from River Plate, and Dirceu, who was joining Verona, felt the same way. We didn't play in the opening match and from that moment the tour was dead, although not officially so until the big black clubs Kaisers Chiefs, Orlando Pirates and Moroko Swallows cancelled fixtures for fear of angering black consciousness movements in Soweto.

My next problem was where to go from South Africa. A planned holiday in the United States had been cancelled because of the tour; I didn't fancy the long flight to Argentina for just a few days there before I had to take off again for France; I hadn't a visa for England; and there was little point in leaving early for Paris when I would see so much of it during the season. So, with more than a week to spare before I had to report to St Germain on 1 August, we decided on a short family break in Spain. Apart from the grounds in Alicante and Barcelona, I'd seen little of the country during the World Cup. We decided to holiday in Marbella – and who should I run into there but Peter Day, the Tottenham secretary. He was on holiday too, and we played golf together. Sylvia, myself and the children mixed as a family with English holiday-makers and found no ill-feeling; everyone was so nice to us and there was no talk of the war. The general friendliness made us long to revisit England.

'It needn't be just a visit, you can go back and play,' said Peter Day, explaining that Tottenham could invalidate the transfer because St Germain hadn't paid the fee on the agreed date. I suspected that the French were hanging on to their money until I passed the club medical, which they had wanted me to take in Paris immediately after the World Cup. The date didn't suit me and I asked for a postponement, explaining that I was honour-bound to return to Argentina with the team. Anyway, this hitch gave Tottenham the right to re-claim me if I changed my mind about not playing in England.

Sylvia and the children pressed me when they heard the news. 'Come on,' they said, 'let's go home to London and see our friends.' I applied to the British Consul in Málaga for visas. His office didn't say yes and didn't say no, but thought the Foreign Office would like to consider some of the statements attributed to me during the war; I was given the impression that they had no intention of hurrying over it.

If visas had been granted on the spot, I doubt if I would have gone through with the move to Paris. I imagine that if I had been reunited with my old Tottenham team-mates and friends I would have told the club: 'Invoke that technicality, cancel the transfer.' It was too late for that, though, when the visa finally came through. I had already been passed by the St Germain doctor, signed the forms, and was away with my new team-mates in Majorca for a pre-season tournament.

Francis Borelli, the club president, was kindness itself. He installed us in a large, luxurious apartment in one of the best quarters of Paris; he found an English school for Pablo and arranged for the club to pay the fees; there was a present for my wife and a BMW car for me – yet, in spite of all that, I was depressed. I regretted leaving Tottenham and felt guilty for my ingratitude towards St Germain. I took my troubles to the president, who was understand-

Following pages: *The World Cup went thataway – back-heeled away from us by such clever Italians as Bruno Conti. He is seen here retaining possession for his team in their 2–1 victory at Barcelona.*

ing, as always. 'By all means go to England for a weekend,' he said, doubtless hoping that a brief visit would clear the homesickness out of my system – as it did for a time. I saw Tottenham's first home match – a 2–2 draw with Luton – and was received rapturously by the club and the crowd.

Two months later I was back playing a match in Britain when the second-round draw of the Cupwinners' Cup paired St Germain against Swansea City. This was towards the end of October 1982, when I was feeling more settled in Paris and happier about my form; I was also anxious to show that I had not gone down in the world by joining St Germain – and I think that point was proved by the ease with which we won both legs for a 3–0 aggregate. John Mahoney, a senior Welsh international, marked me at Swansea, where we won 1–0. Afterwards he told reporters: 'Ossie has lost nothing. Not his touch or his quickness off the mark. Or that little skip or the knack of fending off a challenge with his arms. And, most of all, he still doesn't give the ball away.'

It was a nice tribute from Mahoney, who wasn't to foresee that within two more months I would have lost the most essential quality of a professional – my incentive. I can't blame St Germain for that. I can't blame the players, either. They were always friendly and tried to make me feel at home. The trouble stemmed from an injury to my left hamstring which kept me out for six weeks and left endless time to reflect on the fact that Paris would never mean more than a temporary resting-place and that all of us in the family, even little Federico, missed England more than we had ever expected.

Matters came to a head just before Christmas when St Germain confirmed their intention of signing the Yugoslav international Safet Susic in the New Year. The deal had been blocked since the summer by the Yugoslavian F.A. as a reprisal for their team's poor showing in the World Cup; a similar transfer between Arsenal and the Red Star (Belgrade) midfielder Vladimir Petrovic was delayed for the same reason. The arrival of Susic, a forward or midfielder, would mean three foreigners at the club; but only two can play in the French League. Obviously, Susic would have first claim because I couldn't imagine the management bringing him over in mid-season just to play in the reserves. Kees Kist, a Dutch international striker, would be competing with me for the second place. He had a three-year contract; I was only on a one-year agreement. It was therefore certain he would get preference and I would be in the reserves. I couldn't accept demotion, especially when a first-team place awaited me at Tottenham, so I suggested to Francis Borelli that I should be re-sold to them six months early.

Keith Burkinshaw flew over to negotiate, pausing only to greet me with 'You're overweight, you fat little sod!'

I couldn't deny it. My weight had shot up during my spell on the injured list. 'I'll soon take it off,' I promised.

'You better had, because we want you in the Cup against South-ampton,' he said, meaning on the second Saturday of the New Year – although, in the event, a delay over my international clearance certificate prevented me from playing in the match.

Keith was now working for a new board of directors who had taken over Tottenham a few days previously. They were younger men, eager to make a splash and not quibbling about repaying £50,000 to secure my immediate release.

The Falklands, failure in the World Cup, the South African fiasco, five unsettled months in France – it had been a bad year for me after starting so well, but I felt that rejoining Tottenham meant that things had come right at the end. So I flew home for Christmas in Argentina full of confidence that 1983 would see the clouds roll away.

# 13 WORLD CUP 1982

The best player in the World Cup was not Maradona, as had been expected, or the powerful Falcao of Brazil, or Rummenigge of West Germany with his sudden spurts, or that graceful Frenchman, Platini. In my opinion, all those great stars were outshone by Gaetano Scirea, a technician blessed with superb vision. He was Italy's sweeper and the keystone of their eventual triumph. He was so consistent, he never had a bad match. I rank Scirea even above Paolo Rossi, whose six World Cup goals received extra recognition some months later with his landslide win in the 1982 ballot for European Footballer of the Year. Rossi was sharp, always in position to score the important goals. I was also impressed by the cleverness of winger Bruno Conti, and there cannot be any argument about the genuine class of the midfielders Marco Tardelli and Giancarlo Antognoni. Those five – Scirea, Rossi, Conti, Tardelli and Antognoni – were the stars of a side that beat Argentina, Brazil, Poland and West Germany to win the World Cup. Such results speak for themselves and, being half-Italian myself, I was delighted for the people of Italy, although unable to banish some misgivings about the general quality of the tournament.

I cannot go all the way with the view that it was a mediocre World Cup but there is no denying that there was only one continually brilliant team in the field. Brazil didn't win the title but, in my opinion, they were the most attractive side. Italy were capable of being just as colourful as Brazil but they didn't have enough faith in their skills, which probably explains why they qualified only as the second team in their group and didn't win any of their three first-round matches. I don't suppose anyone fancied them after that, especially in a second-round group with Brazil and Argentina – but that was when the Italians found true world form.

The result that suddenly shortened the betting against them was their 2–1 win against Argentina in Barcelona. We finished the match a man short because Gallego had been sent off for hacking Tardelli. The refereeing was often sub-standard in the World Cup but Mr Rainea of Rumania was right in this case. Gallego deserved to go, but I cannot help saying that he had committed only one foul while Gentile of Italy was getting away with dozens. I wish a camera had tracked Gentile as he marked Maradona. The resulting film would have been an encyclopedia of the professional foul.

Italy's victory tore the World Cup from our hands. Their goals – by Tardelli and Cabrini – came close together after nearly an hour's play. Our reply, a 25-yard free kick by Passarella, came too late for us to save the game. Defeat loads a heavy burden on a side in the second stage of a World Cup, especially in the 1982 tournament where the fixtures had been arranged in a way that left far too much time for the preliminary groups but turned the important final week into a headlong rush. There were too many teams – you don't want twenty-four sides in a World Cup – and too much deference to T.V. schedules. It's a great tournament that should stand on its own feet and not sell out to the cameras.

Anyway, losing to Italy meant that we could have only two days' rest before being flung into action against Brazil. If we had drawn, the Italians would have been obliged to play Brazil first – instead, as 2–1 winners, Italy were able to put their feet up for five days. I don't want to make too much of this disadvantage; in our case, it didn't make a lot of difference because we simply weren't in the form to retain the World Cup, as Brazil showed by beating us 3–1. They took an early lead when Eder's free kick bounced off the crossbar; Zico scored by winning the race for the loose ball. Serginho headed the second from Falcao's lovely chip to the far post and the third goal was a shot from Junior, the attacking left-back. Diaz scored for us in the closing minutes when the match was already lost beyond recall, especially as we had been reduced to ten men

*Following pages: Back in Britain after a six-month absence, I'm seen here playing for Paris St Germain at Swansea in the Cupwinners' Cup. We won 1–0.*

after Maradona had been sent off. He had fouled Brazil's substitute, Batista – a waist-high foul that someone dubbed 'a vasectomy tackle'. You'll remember that crunching challenge by Ricky Villa on a Brazilian in the 1978 World Cup. That was on Batista, who was also the victim of a damaging tackle by Passarella in the 1981 Mundialito in Montevideo. So Batista may feel that he has become a marked man whenever Argentina meet Brazil, but that isn't so. There was no conspiracy to get him – but, like all hard men, he must inevitably find himself taking the stuff he dishes out. There was no premeditation about Maradon's foul on him. It was purely a temperamental reaction to seeing one of our players, Barbas, needlessly floored by Batista in a match that Brazil had already won. I must say that it was also quite uncharacteristic of Maradona who was deeply distressed afterwards when he had cooled down and realized what he had done.

I spent a lot of time with Maradona around the hotels and training camps in Spain. He was on my table, so we ate together every day. I like him because he is highly intelligent but I felt sorry for him, too, on seeing that this great footballer no longer fully enjoys the game. The football he likes best are kick-arounds with his two younger brothers and a bunch of mates, but such uncomplicated pleasures are rare in Maradona's life. There's always another plane to catch, another contract to sign, another meaningless friendly match to play, another personal appearance to make, another interview to give. The price that Diego Maradona paid for riches and world fame at twenty-one was the sacrifice of his youth. He's been in the public eye from boyhood and has never had the chance to be anonymously young and foolish, which is a tragedy because he is not an extrovert but a sensitive kid who would be happier out of the spotlight. It's too late for that now. Maradona today is a corporation, a commodity of which someone always wants something extra. The burden of demands by businessmen and spectators, combined with the lost, irreplaceable years, have made it impossible for him to derive proper satisfaction from his colossal talent. The boy is a worrier. His pre-match nerves throughout the World Cup surprised me. He was scared of personal failure, as are all good professionals to some extent, but he was quite unable to reassure himself with the thought that failure is a comparative word in his case because even an ordinary Maradona performance outshines nearly everyone else at their most brilliant.

That's why a world-record outlay of £7,000,000 was required to move him from Argentina to Barcelona in the summer of 1982. I cannot say 'world record transfer fee' because the deal was not a straightforward transaction between clubs. The clearest indication of its complexity is that the legal fees totalled £125,000. I have converted the sums into sterling for convenience although all the payments were made in United States dollars, the foreign currency best trusted by Argentinian clubs. Argentinos Juniors, his first club in Buenos Aires, received almost £3,000,000. Boca Juniors, the big dockland club who took Maradona on loan when Argentinos could no longer afford his wages, were paid £1,000,000 for their trouble. Various levies and taxes and costs and expenses helped to swell the total, as did the expected receipts from a contract for a Boca v. Barcelona friendly in 1983. The second biggest payment in the transfer was £1,500,000 to Maradona himself as a signing-on fee in addition to his wages of £9,000 a week over a four-year agreement. Who else but Barcelona, with regular home crowds of 120,000, could have afforded such sums?

Maradona reported for duty a month after being sent off in Barcelona for fouling Batista. No one held it against him; indeed, his arrival aroused such fervour that 60,000 people poured into the Nou Camp stadium for his first practice match, which was really just a kick-about with the club's goalkeepers playing as rival centre-forwards. The reason for the enormous support is that F.C. Barcelona represents Catalan nationalism against the Castilians of Madrid. No expense is spared to bring the championship back to Catalonia yet, despite all their celebrated managers and world-class players, Barcelona have won the Spanish League only once in the last twenty years, in 1974, when Johan Cruyff of Holland, fastest and brainiest forward of his era, was Barcelona's spearhead. One title isn't much to show for a history of astronomical expenditure, so there are sudden feuds and disagreements in the boardroom as the managers and superstars come and go. Only the hopes and dreams remain.

Nothing could have been worse for Maradona, in the circumstances, than falling ill with hepatitis at Christmas 1982, with Barcelona only two points behind Real Madrid at the top of the table and the season not halfway through. Hepatitis, a disabling form of jaundice, is dreaded particularly by sportsmen because of its weakening effect, its habit of lingering in the bloodstream and recurring occasionally, and because of the long lay-off required for recovery. Five or six months is not unknown. Maradona, though, had barely taken to his bed before Barcelona fans were being led to expect his return within three months in time for the European Cupwinners' Cup quarter-final against F.C. Austria of Vienna. I know that Barcelona, as a renowned and responsible club, would always be guided by their medical advisers but, at the same time, Mardona cannot fail to be aware of the supporters' wish for a swift come-back. He might feel obliged to play too soon for his own good.

If he takes no risks of that nature, Maradona and Barcelona could be very good for each other, especially now that Menotti has become the club's team-manager. I have a lot of faith in Maradona and I also believe he'll learn how to keep a safer distance from the many commercial distractions that can put a player off his game. It's an area where the Argentina squad failed collectively in the 1982 World Cup. We were the holders and, by common consent back home, the best twenty-two players in Argentina, which spared us from the personal attacks and disputes that accompanied the selection in 1978. We had done roughly the same training that won us the World Cup and, as Spain is the closest country culturally to our own, we were as good as at home again. Yet we failed. We had a good team. I doubt if any impartial judge would have classed us outside the strongest five in the world – we still belong there, in my opinion. Yet we lost three of our five matches. What went wrong?

Defeat in the Falklands has been advanced as a reason, but it's a poor excuse. Set-backs on the battlefield didn't undermine the team. A combination of failings was to blame, but principally that a major-ity of players stopped concentrating on what won the World Cup in the first place. Footballers, once they have reached the top, find it extraordinarily hard to keep their minds on what got them there. Money becomes too great an influence. The bourgeois life beckons. Hangers-on gather. Fellows come into the hotel making presents of expensive shoes and silk shirts. Fat fees are offered for nothing more demanding than dropping in at an advertising party or posing for a few pictures. Another cause of divided attention could have been the number of players – Diaz, Passarella, Kempes, Barbas, Mara-dona, Tarantini and myself among them – who were arranging transfers to new clubs. Personally, I didn't find this affecting my football – indeed, I was more satisfied with my play in Spain than with my performances in 1978 – but I suppose it's possible that the frequent talk of moves created an atmosphere of a team breaking up. A definite distraction was the presence of wives and children in nearby hotels. Some players would have been better if kept completely away from their wives; they should have been thinking about the World Cup instead of being bothered by family trivia.

The World Cup was intended as the highest expression of football but has been turned – and especially so in Spain – into a feast of commercialism. Hucksters and money-men have got hold of it. They would be easy scapegoats for our failure but, to be honest, I don't think that Argentina's dressing-room was the only one infected by the what's-in-it-for-me outlook. So, in the end, I cannot put my finger on exactly what went wrong.

I only know that we were in trouble from the start when, as holders, we opened the World Cup against Belgium at Barcelona. Opening ceremony matches are usually banker draws but we lost this one to a goal by Vandenbergh. It was annoying because I didn't rate the Belgians. I know they were finalists in the 1980 European Championships and I know they went on to win our group, but I considered them a mediocre side with no special qualities and I feel their results in the second round – losing 3–0 to Poland and 1–0 to Russia – show that I'm right. We didn't play well against the Belgians but thought we were good enough to get a draw. The goal in the sixty-second minute wrecked that hope and we became nervous, rushing and hurrying our vain attempts to equalize.

Five days later we put everything right – or imagined that we had – by beating Hungary 4–1 at Alicante. There were two goals by Maradona and one apiece by Bertoni and myself. This was our high-spot of the tournament, the only time when we shaped like world champions. A penalty by Passarella and a goal by Bertoni against El Salvador at Alicante qualified us without further trouble for the second round, but the defeat by Belgium had doomed us into joining the infinitely more powerful of the two second-stage groups. We had to meet Italy and Brazil, instead of the Russians and Poles, but still believed we could get it right and qualify for the semi-finals.

Menotti felt the same way. He expected a change of form that never materialized. Loyalty and optimism are among his most attractive qualities, but they worked against him in Spain and the press in Argentina crucified him for it. Maradona, too, was hammered. It's too easy to say now that Menotti should have made changes; there was no demand for them in the dressing-room at the time. We wouldn't have dreamed of questioning Menotti's judgement but, on reflection, I feel the team lacked a strong character.

I won't make individual criticisms, it's not my way. Eleven of us played, eleven of us failed, eleven of us were guilty. I felt this collective guilt keenly. It was behind my refusal to go to Paris for a medical, instead of returning to Argentina with the team.

We had flown out together so we should fly back together and face the music – but there wasn't any hostility at Buenos Aires airport apart from the customs men impounding our luggage pending the payment of £10,000 in duty. Only our families waited to greet us. The rest of Argentina had other matters on its mind. We were yesterday's men and could be ignored.

England's failure made the World Cup a double disappointment for me. They started by scoring against France at Bilbao in only twenty-seven seconds, thereby winning Bryan Robson a gold watch for the fastest goal in World Cup history, but finished by scoring only once in four and a half hours. Their last three results were 1–0 against Kuwait, 0–0 against West Germany, and 0–0 against Spain. They were a moderate team doing their moderate best and with no policy beyond qualifying for the second round. Ron Greenwood seemed to have convinced himself that England couldn't win the World Cup and were capable only of making a reasonably good impression by winning their opening group; his selection of old, experienced players was accordingly unadventurous. There was no eye to the future, no chance for Glenn Hoddle, the most gifted Englishman, to establish himself in the months before the tournament. No place in the attack for Gary Shaw of Aston Villa or Garth Crooks of Tottenham, no place as the combative all-rounder for Graham Roberts of Tottenham. A lot of footballers left behind must have thought they could have done better than those who went to Spain. If England want to win anything, they'll have to take risks. They have the players to win a World Cup. They could have amazed themselves in Spain.

# 14 COME-BACK

Luton on a wet and windy January afternoon was the scene of my League come-back in 1983. The home crowd booed me as expected, but not as fiercely as I had feared when I was worrying about the match the week before. 'They'll try it on for a time to see if they can unsettle Ossie, but it won't last long,' said Keith Burkinshaw afterwards, adding that he was pleased with my performance on a heavy pitch not really suited to my style.

I was glad to get the game, and the extra attention it attracted, out of the way, and particularly glad to have played a part in the equalizer by Glenn Hoddle who came on as substitute about twenty minutes from the end when we were trailing 1–0. A foul on me gave Glenn his chance. I rolled the free kick back to him and he swerved it round the wall for his first club goal of the season.

It was also the team's first goal for four months in an away League game; a statistic that tells everything about Tottenham's decline in the 1982–3 season. I had a first-hand view of the slump a couple of days later when Burnley, from the relegation zone of the Second Division, beat us 4–1 on our own ground in the Milk Cup. A crazy result, especially as we had been leading 1–0 and looking like certain winners. They equalized out of the blue, and while we were wondering how it happened they scored again and again and again. We were all playing too badly to stop them. There's no other explanation. It wasn't a lack of motivation on our part; of course, it's always easier for the under-dogs to gee themselves up in Cup ties, but this was a quarter-final and we wanted to win it just as keenly as Burnley.

On the day, though, we weren't good enough. We threw it away.

Played three, drew two, lost one – that was the disappointing start to my homecoming. I didn't finish on a winning side until little Terry Gibson (he's an inch smaller than I am) beat two West Bromwich defenders and shot from an angle to score the deciding goal in a fourth-round F.A. Cup tie against West Bromwich.

With the Cup still at White Hart Lane, fans started talking about our chances of becoming the first team this century to win a hat trick of finals. These speculations were stilled within days by a series of injuries. Glenn Hoddle, even after a week of tests and intensive treatment of a damaged ankle, was fit enough to go to Everton for the fifth round only as the substitute. Garry Brooke was in the intensive care unit of a North London hospital after a car crash on the way home from a wedding. He wasn't driving; in fact, he was the middle passenger on the back seat, yet he finished with the most serious injuries, principally six broken ribs. Garry had shot himself into the club records with a hat trick in only six minutes against Coventry City at Tottenham in October 1982. He was also our penalty-taker when in the team, and as the second-highest scorer until his accident, he was a handy player to have around.

I was on the injured list too: I had a broken leg after a tackle by Manchester City's centre-forward David Cross in a 2–2 draw at Maine Road. It was a clumsy challenge by Cross, who had no hope of winning the ball. He caught me on the side of my left shin with his boot – a routine foul with no evil intention and, normally, no risk of real damage. So I was unlucky, and because footballers are an unsentimental lot, I received a fair amount of teasing with the sympathy. One of my favourite sayings was thrown back at me: 'Great players don't get injured.' Keith Burkinshaw, for one, catalogued my injuries over the last three months. There was a thigh strain that resisted treatment in Paris, then a shoulder injury that delayed my come-back with Tottenham, and finally the broken leg. 'What's the matter, Ossie?' he asked. 'I thought great players never got injured!'

My fracture wasn't a bad one, just a crack in the bone, and I set myself the target of returning within two months. I took great pride in discarding my crutches as quickly as possible while trying to walk without a limp, which I did in just over a fortnight.

So I was fit to travel with the team as a spectator to Everton where we were trying to set a record of nineteen unbeaten F.A. Cup ties.

It wasn't to be, of course. We had too many injuries, so that we could never put out the same team twice. On the day, we were rightly beaten 2–0 by Everton's effort and physical challenge.

The road home is always longer for a losing side, and I had plenty of time to think on the 200-mile drive back from Merseyside. My stiff leg and a series of defeats were the evidence for saying that the return to Tottenham hadn't been the cinch that everyone expected but, in spite of everything, I was glad to be back. I swept season 1982–3 right out of my mind and told myself that Tottenham would take off again next August.

I know I can still do my stuff in England for a few more seasons. I don't see any immediate prospect of needing to hit the trail to my retirement ranch some sixty miles from Córdoba. It's called El Pitón (The Python) and is small by Argentinian standards, but the 1,000 acres are enough to support 400 head of cattle and keep me busy when the day comes to hang up my boots.

Thirty-one is the age when every footballer starts planning for retirement. The dreaded day comes up faster than any of us expect. You see a kid in the reserves or youth team and tell yourself: 'Why, he's not fit to lace my boots!' But youngsters develop fast. Inside a year, the kid is challenging you for your place. One day you look at the team-sheet and find he's got it. That's how it has been for almost every player in history and I'll be no exception, but I can go with no regrets, warmed by memories of having been at the top playing alongside great players in great teams on great occasions from River Plate to Wembley.

# INDEX